Mary Woodson

The title

Justice were never services-
In the death of a simple man

July

I dedicate this book to my mother, who gone on. She inspired me to continue a work she had begun. I would like to also compliment my family members who gave me support and love. There were times when I was hurting and the Lord gave me strength to finish this book. I would like to acknowledge my grandmother, who was devoted to her daughter when she was hurting. I watched my mother cry many days about her son; it hurt her to talk about her son's death.

I thank all the people who took their time and sat down with me to talk about my brother's death. Before I completed the book, I regret I never had a chance to talk to some people who are deceased. I also thank people who didn't want to talk about it. There some I never had a chance to talk to. I never pressured anyone. For whatever reason they had, I understand. I truly thank everyone. There were tears in their eyes when they talked about his death because they were there and seen it all.

I thank Pee Wee and his brother Frank Jr. for their support, even though Frank Jr. was not living there at the time of my brother's death. I thank Rev. O.D. Robinson and his family, who witnessed it all. I thank my brother and his wife Geraldine for assisting me with important facts and details. I thank Mr. George W. Spear who gone on for his information. And also I thank Mr. Amos M. Pates, who encouraged me to document this information in the form of a book.

This is a true story of Willie Woodson Jr., my older brother, and how he was shot and killed by the Mississippi Highway Enforcement. He was shot one hundred and fifty times or more. His body was torn up by their bullets, and justice was never done. He died at the age of 22. I couldn't imagine him dead at that young age. I want the world to know how my brother died and how his life was taken by man. And how my family was treated after his death. The words were out how the Mississippi law enforcement bragged about how they killed them a nigger in Mound Bayou, Mississippi.

My parented birthed twelve children, eight boys and four girls, of which nine are alive today. The deceased siblings, along with my parents and grandmother, are as follows: my father Willie died June 10, 1965; my mother Millie died March 2, 1991; our grandmother Annie died December 3, 1996; my sister Dorothy died March 2, 2007; and my brother Joe died Oct 27, 2007.

In 1967, I started composing this story about my brother's death because my mother asked me to write a book about how he was brutally murdered. His body was perforated by the impact of 150 bullets that were the cause of his death. It took me years to complete this story because its contents were filled with pain and emotional hurt. Members of the family and other people felt the pain as they remember his tragic death as I gathered my detail for this book. There were days my mother didn't wanted talk about her son because she was in pain. I didn't want to bother my mama too much because it hurt her dearly. Emotionally, she was still in pain from the tragedy of his death, which constantly brought tears to her eyes. She discussed in detail as many things as she could remember about his life and death.

My mother passed before I could finish his story. I needed more because of the painful past. Another person who was hurt by his death was my grandmother. She refused to talk about it. In order to retrieve information, I had to talk to my brother. C.J. gave me an abundance of information, but it was an on-and-off basis. C.J. and Jim had a great relationship as brothers, and C.J. was present at his death. Joe was not there when Jim was killed. And Earnest did not associate with Jim that much because he was much younger. As the result, this was all the retrieved detailed information that was needed to complete the book.

Before I begin, let me say this: we all were born in the country, in a different town.

Willie Woodson Jr. was born February 22, 1943, in Utica, Mississippi. He was named after his father. We all called him by his nickname, Jim or June. Some people even called him by his real name.

My mother remembered little about his childhood. She recalled that Jim was a good baby and didn't cry much. It really hurt Mama to talk about his past because it was very difficult to describe his life. Mama said his daddy spoiled him. She remembered June when he was four years old. He stayed home and babysat his little brothers, Joe and C.J., while she and Daddy worked in the cotton field. They didn't have a babysitter.

When they came home from work every day, everything was in place. Mama said they didn't have any problem out of them. Mama said that June was a quiet child and liked being by himself a lot. Few time he got into a little trouble fighting with his little brother Joe. Mama said Joe would always start the fight between him and June. Mama said one day Joe got on June's nerves, and he struck him and nearly knocked him out. He got a whipping for that and didn't want to fight with Joe again. Mama recalled June was a very smart child, and he love to follow his daddy around. At that point, Daddy started taking June to work with him on the farm. Mama said June loved feeding the cows and riding the horses. Daddy was the owner of those animals.

Another time Jim got into mischief was when mama took the boys fishing. Mama recalled that June and Joe were running around the pond playing while she was sitting down fishing. June grew tired and wanted to stop playing. June told Mama to tell Joe to leave him alone. She warned Joe to stop playing with him. She kept telling Joe to leave him alone. Joe didn't stop, and he got pushed off into the water. If Mama hadn't reached for him in time, he would have drowned.

Daddy whipped June when he got home from work for his mischief. Mama remembered that Daddy was aware of June's quick temper. She shared her thought with Daddy. The two of them thought that Jim would possibly hurt Joe when he grew tired of him and didn't want to be bothered. Mama said that lots of time Joe would aggravate Jim not knowing that he wanted to be left alone.

Mama said that when June was at the age of six, Daddy would take him to the cotton field and teach him how to pick cotton and chop it. And he even tough him how to drive a tractor and a truck. He didn't have much trouble out of him.

Jim knew how to drive from earlier training by his dad. One day while Daddy was gone and Mama was in the kitchen cooking dinner, Jim got his daddy's keys. He drove up and down the road having a good time. Joe came into the house and told Mama that Jim was in Daddy's truck. Mama rushed outside and made him bring the truck home. She took the keys and whipped his butt.

Another incident was when Mama said that one night while they were asleep, Jim came into their room and went under Daddy's pillow. He removed his gun, carried it back into his room, and placed it under his pillow. When Daddy woke up the next morning and reached for his gun, it was missing and he thought Mama had taken it. She told him that she hadn't touched his gun, and he went straight to June. June confessed and told Daddy that he had taken the gun. He got a whipping that time, and Daddy told him he'd better not catch his hands on a gun again. My parents never found out why June had taken the gun.

Mama said June loved to help her clean up and wash dishes and hang out the clothes. Mama's memories about Daddy were of a good husband. He was a hardworking man who took care of his family. He made money running his juke joint and farming. Mama and her mother helped Daddy out in his juke joints by cooking, and selling food, beer, and corn whisky.

Mama said Daddy and her never argued or fought with each other. He never wanted her to work. He wanted her to stay home with the kids. He took care of his family. They moved from one place to another so often. That's why some of us were born in different towns. Mama said that Daddy didn't like staying in one place too long.

He also expressed the difficulty of growing up without parents. His parents died when he was a child, and life was very rough. He was raised by his three sisters. Daddy met Mama while he was serving in the army. Mama said Daddy talked to June about obeying his parents and explained to him how he was raised without a parent. He taught June how to work and take of himself. He also taught him how to be independent. He stressed the importance of not letting anyone push him around. That meant not taking mess off anyone. In general he told June not to argue with people because arguments provoke people.

Most of all, he taught him how to fight and not to be a loser. June learned a lot whenever he was with Daddy. Jim loved his parents and never talked back to them. Daddy told June he was not always going to be around. June listened to Daddy and took his advice.

Constantly on the move, Daddy gave up a lot of things and moved to another town quite often. He didn't want his family hurt. We moved to Shaw, Mississippi. Daddy opened up another juke joint with his close friend Jeff. Mama and Grandmother ran the kitchen. Joe had to stay home with the other kids. During that time, C.J. said that Jim would get into those people's cars and drive them. When he got caught, he got a beating.

We lived on a man's plantation, and he did work for that man. Daddy and the man fell out with each other though, and Daddy wanted to move away from Shaw because he did not get along which his boss man. Mama said that Daddy told her that he was going to live in Shelby, Mississippi. While preparing to move, the boss man found out and told Daddy that he wasn't going anywhere. To enforce it, he said that the man threatened him and his family.

Daddy told Mama that he was not going to let that man hurt him or his family. So Daddy packed all our things and told Mama what time we were going to move off that man's place.

I recall this incident. I was a little girl and remember a little about that night. Daddy had one of those big red trucks with a bed on it. It was around midnight. I saw them putting some things on the truck, and when we got ready to leave I got in the front seat with Mama and Daddy. The other six children were in the back of the truck.

When we got ready to leave out, Daddy drove down the road without any lights on because he did not want anyone to see us leave. When we got on the highway heading north, Daddy looked in his rearview mirror and saw someone following him. He pulled out his gun and, passing it to Mama, told her to hold on to it. I can remember Daddy telling Mama to sit back, and then he put his foot on the gas and picked up speed to leave that truck way behind. When Daddy didn't see the truck behind him anymore, he turned off on another road. Quietly, we sat there for a few minutes because my daddy wanted to know who was following him. Finally, the truck passed by and Daddy recognized that it was his boss man who was following him. As a result, Daddy went in another direction. In their conversation, Daddy told Mama that he would have done something to the boss man if he had hurt his family. At last, we drove into Shelby, Mississippi.

My parents were loving and caring people. My daddy didn't drink any alcohol, but he smoked cigarettes. He was a quiet man. I have seen my daddy come home and put all his money into Mama's hand. He didn't keep a lot of money on him. He made sure he kept food on the table and clothes on our backs. He was there for his family. As a matter of fact, he was there when Mama gave birth to all her children. He was there to deliver some of us. We didn't have that much, but we had each other. My mother was a beautiful woman. She did not drink, smoke cigarettes, or party. She loved going to church. She made sure that we were there with her on Sunday morning. My daddy loved helping people, no matter what of type of problem they were having. He was there for them. One thing he did was that he didn't take any mess. He was not afraid of anyone.

When we lived in Shelby, Jim, Joe, and C.J. attended school there. It was one day. This was the incident that shortened their stay. In the classroom, it was said that Jim was looking under a little girl's skirt with a mirror on the floor by her desk. He was accused of it, but he really didn't do it. It was another person who did it, but Jim was blamed. He was expelled that day after school. After school that day on their way home, Jim saw the little girl and walked up to her. They had words. Joe said that Jim asked the little girl why he was lied on. She walked away from him, and he walked up to her and stuck her in the back with a pencil. She ran home crying. He came home and told Daddy what had happened. Joe also told daddy that he didn't believe Jim did look under the girl's dress and repeated that she lied on him.

The next morning, Daddy took Jim back to school to straighten things out with the girl's parents. It turned out ugly. They wanted to arrest him and kick him out of school, but Daddy told them they weren't going to do anything to his son. He expressed his anger, telling them that he didn't want his son in that school anymore. Daddy apologized to the little parent. He took Jim out of that school and transferred him to the school in Mound Bayou, Mississippi. Mama said she wanted to move from Shelby to Mound Bayou after she had her baby.

I recall once when my mother was pregnant with her child, Daddy had just got in from work and Mama wanted something from the store so she could cook dinner for the family. Daddy was tired after he had come home from work. We all left to go with Daddy. Jim, Joe, C.J., Earnest, and me. We were all sitting in the front seat with Daddy in his 1954 green Chevy pickup. Daddy drove up to town to Shelby to the grocery store.

On our way back home, when Daddy got ready to turn into our driveway, he threw out his left hand and was stuck from behind by another truck. This impact knocked Daddy's truck all the way off the road with his arm hanging out. The collision turned our truck over three times or more with us in it. Daddy was thrown from his truck and we were all inside. We were not hurt but afraid.

People stopped to see if anyone was hurt. The police and firemen helped us out of the truck, but Daddy was really hurt. I remember seeing them take Daddy in the house and lay him across the bed. Because he was in pain, they rushed him to the hospital. He was there for a couple of weeks. I don't remember what hospital they took him to. His injuries were a fractured hip along with other problems. When he came home from the hospital, he got better and started back to work.

When we lived in Mound Bayou, it was in the country. We lived on Mr. Dennis Moody's place. He was a well-known black businessman who owned a lot of property. He and his wife owned a grocery store that Earnest and I worked in. They were very nice people. They let people have groceries on credit until they got paid. Daddy and Mr. Moody were good friends. We picked cotton and chopped for him. At the age of 13 years old, Daddy got Jim a job driving a tractor for Mr. Moody. He also drove their truck around to pick up people who worked in the cotton fields. At the end of the day, he would return them to their home. We all had to go to the field to chop and pick cotton. Our sister Dorothy was an exception because of illness. Mr. Moody let Daddy use one of his houses to open up a juke joint. Daddy did a lot of work for Mr. Moody and his wife.

Though he worked few jobs, Daddy worked as a policeman in Mound Bayou at one time. They all worked with the NAACP along with Martin Luther King and Mr. Amize Moore, Dennis Moody, Tommy Heron, and George Brooks, who owned a juke joint in Mound Bayou. There were other black businesses in Mound Bayou, run by people who loved helping people get food and clothes for their families. They also helped other community projects.

Between 1956 and 1957, Daddy used one of Mr. Moody's houses to distribute food and clothes to the needy. He had lot of support. People came from everywhere to receive food and clothes. Daddy gave many things away free. People started breaking into the place and started stealing clothes and food. Daddy soon closed the place down. His juke joint was kept open for a while.

I remember Mr. Moody had a fishing pond. He allowed people to go in and fish, but not to swim. As children, we caught fish and snakes. We would drop our poles and take off running.

One day Mama and Daddy had to leave the house. They specifically told us not to go down to the fishing pond. Jessie, T.W., and Earnest went down to the pond to swim but not to fish. When Daddy came home and they were not in the house, he immediately walked down to the fishing pond and caught them swimming. When they saw Daddy coming after them, they rushed out of the water and tried to run. Daddy caught them and whipped their butts all the way back to the house. When they got inside the house, he whipped their butts again.

The plan we devised when we received punishment was the addition of more clothing. When my brothers did something wrong and Daddy found about it, they would go and put on at least two or three pairs of pants. This was done to keep the licks from hurting them. It worked for a while, but Daddy caught on to what they were doing because they were not feeling those licks. He would make them pull off some of the clothing. C.J., Dorothy, and I never did get whippings. Jim and Joe did not get many whippings either.

When Jim got a job, Daddy would let him keep his money. He showed him how to buy his own clothes, shoes, and personal things. Jim loved to shop for himself and keep his appearances up. He didn't like for anyone to mess with his things. Joe and Jim got into a couple of fights because Joe messed with his things.

Jim lost his job working for Mr. Moody. Someone said that he and Joe went into Mr. Moody's house and took his gun. Jim's name was involved. So Mr. Moody believed that Jim and Joe had broken into his house and taken money and the gun. As a result, Jim and Mr. Moody got into an argument. Daddy questioned Jim and Joe, and they told him it wasn't them who broke into Mr. Moody's house. Daddy made Jim quit that job, and he found Jim another job. Jim drove tractor for another person.

That's what Jim loved doing. He enjoy driving tractor and working on a farm, picking and chopping cotton. He learned how to drive various types of farm equipment. When he got paid, he did not waste his money on whisky and beer because he did not drink. He picked good friends to be with. Daddy let him got out with his friends during the week and some weekends. Everybody knew each other. They were too young to drink beer and whisky. They all hung out most of the time around George Brook's place. At that place, they watched television, listened to music, and danced. He loved to have fun by telling jokes and playing cards. Jim was a fun type of person and had many friends.

When summer came around, he wanted to go and visit his cousin in Slaughter, Mississippi. Daddy took him down to Slaughter to stay with my great grandmother. He enjoyed playing with his cousins. He got into a fight while working in the cotton field. The big fight was when someone stole his sack of cotton. My great grandmother could not handle him. No one could handle him. She wrote Daddy a letter and told him to come and get Jim. So Daddy had to go and get him. Jim did not let anyone get the best of him because he remembered the things Daddy had taught him.

Jim stood his ground when it came to fighting. C.J. said that Jim got into a fight with Terry Levy and whipped his butt. They had to pull Jim off that young man. Another time, Jim got into a fight with a little white boy named Van. His father, Mr. Van Skelton, was very well known in Mound Bayou. His son shot Jim with a BB gun, and Jim jumped on him and beat him up. The little boy got away and ran home to tell his daddy that Jim jumped on him. Jim went to his father and did the same. He told Daddy about the incident and what he had done to the little boy and why.

Mr. Skelton came to the house because he was very upset at what Jim had done to his son. He told Daddy that he didn't want Jim playing with his son anyone. Daddy told him that his son shot Jim with a BB gun. Mr. Skelton threatened Jim, and Daddy jumped in and said that nobody was going to mess with his son. Then Mr. Skelton walked away. I don't remember if Jim had anything to do with him.

Jim knew Daddy was on his side. C.J. recalled that Daddy always told him and Joe to keep their eyes on Jim because it was going to be hard for anyone to whip him when he had to defend himself. Jim didn't like anyone helping when he fought. He never bragged about himself.

He never thought of himself as being tough. He was a nice person and tried to get alone with everyone.

Every Sunday morning, we all went to Sunday school with or without Mama and Daddy. Dorothy and I sang in the church choir. Jim, Joe, and C.J. were all baptized in a small church in Mound Bayou in 1958, I believe. Jim found happiness in going to church when he was a young man. Mama and Daddy had no problem out of him in going to Sunday school.

I remember one day when Mama, Daddy, Joe, Jim, and C.J. were gone, and they left Dorothy in charge. And Daddy told us we better not leave the house and do what Dorothy told us to do. We were outside in the backyard playing. I saw Earnest go into the house and come back out before walking over to where Dorothy was sitting. She was alone. He walked over and said something to her. I turned my back, and I heard her call out my name. Mary, Mary. I looked around, and her hair was on fire. I ran and got a bucket of water that was sitting beside the house and threw it all over her head to put the flame out. The flame did not get to her face because I put it out in time. The flame just burned all her hair off her head. Dorothy always had very long hair that fell halfway down her back.

I told Earnest that I was going to tell Daddy when he got home. He was afraid and wanted me to promise him that I would not tell Daddy and Mama that he did it. I told him that Dorothy would be the one to tell it. In the meantime, he went and put on a couple of pairs of pants. When Mama and Daddy walked in the door, Dorothy ran to Mama and told her what Earnest had done to her hair. Daddy was very upset and went looking for Earnest, who was outside hiding under the house. Daddy found out where he was hiding and made him come out from under there. Daddy went and got his switch and tore his butt up. Earnest was crying and screaming from those hurtful licks. Then Daddy noticed that tears were not coming from his eyes and that Earnest had on three pair of pants. He quickly made him pull the pants off. He continued whipping Earnest by putting his head between his legs. This time he tore his butt up and real tears fell from Earnest. Mama had to stop Daddy from whipping him. She was very upset about Dorothy's hair, which never grew back long like it was previously.

One day when Mama, Daddy, Jim, Joe, C.J., Earnest, and I were all out in the field cotton field, I was the water girl, taking water to the people. We were all chopping cotton side by side each other, and Daddy make sure we didn't get behind. He would help us to catch up. Earnest asked Daddy if he could go to the bathroom. Daddy gave him permission to go but not to stay too long. The time passed, and Earnest did not returned, so Daddy got worried and went looking for him. He found him hanging around with Joe, C.J., and another worker. Daddy made them to go back to work. When Earnest saw Daddy coming, he ran back to his cotton row and picked up his hoe to start back chopping cotton. When Daddy came back to his row, he picked up his hoe and hit Earnest across the back. Earnest screamed and fell to his knees. Daddy made him get up and go back to work as people looked and laughed. Joe and C.J. laughed to see what Daddy had done. Mama told Daddy that he should have been ashamed of himself. Daddy told her that Earnest needed to do what he was told to do. For rest of the day, Earnest didn't do anything wrong. He stayed beside Daddy until everyone got off work.

Daddy never did allow his children to go to clubs or parties. One thing he was afraid of was that Jim would get into a fight with someone. Whenever Jim was up town or at George Brook Club, Daddy was always go around to make sure Jim didn't get into any trouble. He knew Jim had a quick temper, and he would fight if he had to.

As soon Jim turned fourteen years old, his style of entertainment was found in clubs and parties. One night, there was a party going on over at one of his friend's houses. He asked Daddy if he could go and was told no.

After Daddy was gone, he asked Mama and she told him yes. Jim got dressed and left the house. He told Mama that he would be back before Daddy came back. She told him he should hurry back. He also took Daddy's gun from his little black box without anyone knowing it

He was gone for a long time. Daddy came and told Mama that someone told him that Jim was had been seen at a party. He told Mama that he definitely told Jim to stay at home and not to go to the party. He was very upset because Jim didn't do what he was told to do. Daddy really got upset when he look into the little black box and found out one of his guns was missing, and he told Mama that Jim had taken it from his iron box. He didn't want him with his gun because he might hurt someone. He told Mama that he was going to whip him for leaving the house and taking his gun. Mama didn't say a word.

Daddy sat in the rocking chair and waited for him to come home. Jim had really intended to be back before Daddy got back. I was hoping Jim would hurry up and come home. I nervously started walking around the room because and I couldn't go to sleep. The other children were in their rooms sound asleep. My sister Dorothy was in her bed next to mine, and she was asleep. Around nine o'clock, someone knocked on my window. I got up to look out the window and saw it was Jim telling me to go and unlock the back door. I looked into the living room and saw Daddy sleeping. Mama was in the bedroom.

When Jim tried to sneak in the back door without anyone seeing him, he had no idea that Daddy was sitting up waiting on him. Daddy heard Jim come in the back, and I went back in my room to see what daddy was going to do to him. He talked for a few minutes and reached for his switch. He then threw Jim down to his knees and started whipping him. Mama came out of her room telling Daddy to leave him, but he didn't stop. Jim was saying that he was sorry and wouldn't do it again. He was crying and talking at the same time. Mama continued to beg Daddy to stop and leave him alone.

I kept walking around my room and crying because I thought Daddy was going to hurt Jim. I heard Daddy constantly telling Jim that he should never put his hand on his gun again. Daddy kept hitting Jim across his back and butt as he tried to get away. I felt sorry for Jim. I dared not say anything to my father while he was angry. Mama was still screaming that Daddy should leave him alone.

I became afraid and opened my window to crawl out. I hid under the house. I could still hear my father telling Jim that he should never touch his gun again. Then Mama came into my room and noticed that the window was open and I was gone. I could hear her calling my name while I was under the house. I refused to answer. She went back and told Daddy that I wasn't in my room. Daddy left Jim alone. Both parents started looking for me. Jim called out my name, but I refused to answer while under the house. They knew I was not gone very far. They could not see me under the house because it was dark outside. Yet they continued to call my name while I refused to answer.

Finally, I answered them. I came from under the house and we all went back inside to go to bed. Jim went to his room. I went in to check on him to see if he was all right. I saw him lying across the bed on his back crying. I talked to him for a minute and told him not to cry, that everything was going to be alright, and I went to bed.

Sometime during the night while we were sleeping, Jim packed his clothes in a pillow case and left home. Daddy woke up the next morning and went into Jim's room to wake him up.

He wanted Jim to go somewhere with him. He didn't find Jim in his room. My parents began to worry because they had no idea where he could run off to. Daddy took Joe along with him to look for Jim. Daddy went to his sister Eliza's, but she hadn't seen him either. Somewhere Daddy found out where Jim was.

The next morning we all left with Daddy to go to Slaughter where my great grandmother lived. We found him there. He said he caught the Greyhound bus down there. He wanted to stay for the summer. With Daddy's permission, he was given a couple more weeks. He was back by the time the school year began.

One Friday night at Daddy's juke joint when Jim was 14 years old, everybody was sitting around and having fun drinking beer and whisky and playing music and dancing. Daddy was in the other room where they were gambling. Mama and Grandmother were in the kitchen fixing food for the people. She had run out of floor. She wanted me and Joe to drive to the house and bring back flour and meal. Daddy let Joe use his green 1957 Plymouth pickup truck. Joe was 13 years old at that time. Daddy told Joe to go and come back.

On our way to the house, Joe began speeding around the curves. I was telling him that he needed to slow down, but it was too late. The car went out of control and landed in a ditch. My face was slammed against the dashboard, and my nose fractured. Joe did not know what to do. He became scared and worried about what Daddy was going to do to him. My face swelled up badly. Joe told me not to tell Daddy or Mama about what had really happened but to say that I had slipped and fell on my face.

Joe couldn't get the car out of the ditch. We sat there until someone came along. A man stopped by and helped us get the car out of the ditch. The car wasn't damaged at all. We got back on the road and drove on to the house. Joe begged me not to tell Daddy or C.J. I told him that he was going to find out anyway. I didn't know my face was swollen so badly until I looked in the mirror. C.J. started laughing at me and asked Joe what happen to my face, and Joe told him that he went off the road into a ditch. Joe got what Mama had sent us after and drove back to the place.

Daddy was standing on the porch worried about us because we were gone a long time. When I got out of the car, Daddy saw my face and asked Joe what had happened. Joe told him that he had run off the road into a ditch. Daddy checked the car out and saw no damage, and then he walked over to Joe and slapped him. Joe fell to ground. Daddy ordered him to get up and get into the car. He took Joe back home.

I went on into the place and gave Mama the flour and meal and told her what had happened. I got me a milk carton crate and sat by the door to watch people dance and play music.

After a while, Jim came in and surprised us. We didn't know he was coming home. He came over and hugged me and questioned me about what had happened to my face. I told him that Joe had an accident on the way home. He asked about Joe's whereabouts and if he was okay. I told him that I was fine and also Joe, and I said that Daddy had taken Joe home. He went into the kitchen to see Mama and Grandmother. They were surprised to see him. He asked Mama about Daddy and was able to find him. Daddy was surprised to see him.

Jim came back into the café and sat down at the bar with his friends. They began to watch people dance and enjoy music. A big and fat lady came from outside and went over to the juke box to play a song, and she began dancing alone. She must have weighed 300 pounds. When her music went off, Jim got up and went to play his song. Jim asked the woman for a dance. Together the two of them danced a slow dance. He played another song, and the people got so excited that they challenged each other to pick the best dancer. Jim did dance called the slop. He had learned to do this dance while he was out of town. So, they put their money. Some of them made bets on Jim and some on the lady. When the music began to play and they started dancing, everybody stopped what they were doing to watch them. Mama and Grandmother stopped what they were doing and came out of the kitchen to watch them. The best dancer was Jim. He won the money.

A man named Mr. Hick got up from his seat and started walking around with a whisky bottle in his hand. He began cursing. Jim stopped dancing and asked the man to respect his Daddy's place and other people. Mr. Hick said something smart to Jim and cursed him. Jim grabbed the man and hit him so hard and fast that the man stumbled backwards and fell right on me. I was knocked off the milk carton crate. Jim rushed over where I was sitting and pulled the man off me. He threw him out on the porch, and he picked him up again and threw him on the ground. He jumped down on the man and started kicking him all over. His friend, June Lane, tried to pull Jim off the man. Jim told him he didn't need any help. June Lane got back and left him alone. Somehow Mama and Grandmother came out of the place and tried to make Jim leave the man alone. Their effort was of no good. Then somebody went and got Daddy. Daddy made Jim leave the man alone. He separated the two. At that point, Jim didn't exchange any words and stood back like Daddy told him.

Lying there unconscious, Daddy got somebody to take the man to the hospital. Daddy got the report back that the man had a broken rib, a broken arm, and cuts over his eye. He received thirteen stitches over his eye. Mama said that Daddy paid the man's hospital bill. Daddy soon closed the place because people started breaking in.

I remember when he lived on Mr. Dennis Moody's place that this man going around selling ice, and he stopped by our house to see if Mama needed some ice. While she was buying from the man, my sister Dorothy went in the man's truck and took the man's money off his seat without anyone seeing her. The man went to get change for the people, and his money was gone. He accused Jim. The man and Mama got into an argument, and Mama told him her son didn't steal and he didn't taken the money. The man called the police on Jim, and they wanted to take him to jail. Mama questioned Dorothy, and she had the man's money. When Daddy came home, Mama told him what had happened and Daddy went to the man. He told him not to ever come near his house again.

In 1959, we moved from Mr. Moody's place and started living in one of Mr. George Brook's houses. We were close to town and walking distance from school.

Daddy found Jim another job driving tractor for a white man. Joe would go on the job and hang with him. One day Jim brought Joe home. He was driving fast across the railroad track. His speeding caused Joe to fall off the trailer. He was knocked unconscious. Jim looked back and did not see Joe. He turned the tractor around and went back, and he found Joe lying unconscious. He picked Joe up and brought him home. He told mama that Joe was dead. They got Joe to wake up. When Jim went back to work, the boss man was waiting for him. He was very upset because Jim left the job. And he was very upset because he thought Jim had gone in his house and taken his gun. They got into an argument. Jim told the man he did not take his gun. The man cursed Jim, and Jim didn't like his remark. Jim hit the man upside his head and knocked him down to the ground. Jim broke his finger and the man fired Jim, but the man did not press any charges. Daddy talked to the man and apologized for his son.

Jim told Daddy he did not take the man's gun but he did admit that he hit the man. Daddy told him one day he might not be around to keep him out of trouble. Jim did not let anyone get the best of him and he never lost a fight.

When he turned 16 years old, he began smoking cigarettes. He never let Mama or Daddy see him smoke. He never did drink beer or whisky. One day he left his cigarettes at home. He had one left in the pack. Joe found his cigarettes and smoked the last one up. Later, Jim came home and wanted to smoke. He looked for his cigarettes and asked Joe if he had seen his cigarettes. Then Joe told him that Dorothy had smoked up his last cigarette. Dorothy told Jim that she didn't do it and Joe was the one who smoked his last cigarette. Jim let the whole situation go by. He left it alone. But Joe got smart with his mouth and kept the incident up. Mama and Grandmother stood nearby. They tried to get Joe to shut up. Joe thought he was tough. Jim really did not want to fight him until he was hit in the chest by Joe. Jim hit Joe and knocked him right over where Mama and Grandmother were sitting. Joe fell right in Mama's lap. Jim grabbed Joe, and they began to fight furiously. Mama and Grandmother tried to pull them apart. I ran to the screen door and held it open for Joe to run out of the house. I kept telling Joe to run. It was hard for him to get away from Jim. He had a hold on Joe, and he couldn't get away. Mama and Grandmother wrestled with those boys. Finally, Joe got away and ran out the door down into the cotton field. Jim went and took Daddy's gun off the wall. He shot at Joe. Joe kept running until he was out of sight. Joe ran all the way over to Daddy's sister Eliza's house. He stayed there until Daddy came home and picked him up.

When Daddy came home, Mama told him what had happened. The fight was over a cigarette. Daddy had to talk to with both of them. They never fought each other again. He told Joe that he better not ever catch a cigarette in his mouth again. Jim didn't like fighting his brother unless he really had to. He only fought when someone messed with him.

Another time Jim, Joe, C.J., and some of their friends got together and went to Mr. George's place. They sat around and watched television. Mr. George didn't allow them to drink, so they sat and watched other people play music and dance. While they were sitting there, a young man came in from another town and started messing with Jim. He told Jim that he had heard about his reputation in street fighting and how tough he was. C.J. said Jim sat there and didn't say a word. Jim didn't like what the young man was saying to him. Mr. George told them to take it outside. They went outside near the street while the young man was still running off at the mouth. Jim hit the young guy so fast and quick that the guy stumbled and fell to the ground. The guy jumped up and jumped into his car along with his friend. As he drove off, he yelled that he would be back. Actually, he never came back.

Another time, Jim got into a fight with one of Mr. Evans' sons. I don't remember what it was about, but anyway I heard the young man started the fight. Jim hit the young guy in the face and broke his nose. Later they became good friends. Jim never did like fighting with people he knew. He tried to get along with everybody. They came to him with their mess.

There were other people who talked about how tough Jim was, but they did not mess with him. He didn't pick fights with anybody, and he didn't argue with people in general. We heard about guys who wanted to come in and take over Mound Bayou. The guys in Mound Bayou were not going to let them come in and take over where they lived. Jim felt that no one out there could handle him. He also felt that those guys from other towns were afraid to come to Mound Bayou because of his reputation. When Jim showed up, they took off running. Jim was not the tough guy in Mound Bayou. A few of them tried to handle him, but they couldn't. When it came to fighting, Jim did not fight with many of those guys around Mound Bayou unless he had to. It was only when he was forced to. Sometimes he fought to defend himself because he did not want anyone to hurt him.

He had a very quick temper, and he didn't like to argue. He had a good heart. He didn't take anything from his friends. He never stole from his family. These are all the things I remember about my brother and how he live his life.

He was known to hit a person so quick and fast in order to avoid being hit first. He wasn't going to let anyone get the first lick in. His strategy was to hit you first so you would be on the ground before you knew it. That's how he was. His daddy taught him how to fight. He was a nice person and never tried to hurt anyone unless he had to. He never talked to a woman or put his hand on her. There was one woman in Mound Bayou who he was crazy about, though he never messed around with lots of women.

He never got drunk or high off anything. He didn't eat that much. He didn't talk badly about anybody or to anyone. He loved to have fun with his friends. Sometimes he wrestled with them, played cards and told jokes and had everybody laughing. He loved playing football, also.

His friends would ask him who taught him to fight so well. He told him that his daddy taught him. Jim had a good, giving heart. He would also help you to fight if you couldn't handle a person. He had many friends and loved hanging around with them. He wore nice clothes and kept his shoes shined. He dressed very neatly and kept a nice haircut. He never asked Daddy for anything. He wanted to make his own money. He went to the cotton field and picked four to five pounds of cotton a day. He picked three or four rows at a time. My mama gave him money when he didn't have any. My brother, he wasn't mean to us, nor did he whip us. He always gave us money when he was working. C.J. and Jim never argued or fought with each other. The only person who did that was Joe when he thought he was tougher than Jim.

Jim didn't like sitting around. He loved making money and always talked about working. He didn't ask people for anything. He loved having his own. I remember one day out in the cotton field, Jim left his cotton sack to use the restroom. When he came back, he noticed someone had stolen his sack. He went looking for his sack, found out who had stolen his cotton, and went after that person. He beat that person's butt, and Daddy had to leave his cotton sack to pull Jim off that guy. People believed in taking a cotton sack. When Jim worked in the field, he didn't like talking to anyone. That was just the way he was. Although Jim could pick a lot of cotton, he never out-picked Daddy.

Jim tried to stay out of trouble. He was one of those people who couldn't avoid trouble. He had a very quick temper and was quick to fight. That's just the way he was. Although he tried to avoid fighting, he wasn't successful.

Daddy didn't want him to quit school. He wanted him to complete his education. He saw that Jim had a lot of problems in school. He was failing his grade. Daddy and Mama had to go to school almost every day because he had gotten into a fight with somebody. In the 1959 academic school year, Jim dropped out of school. My parents didn't want him to drop out, but the school system kept kicking him out and expelling him for fighting and playing and shooting hooky from school. He wasn't making the grades academically either. It seemed like every day he got into a verbal fight with Daddy about going to school. My father told my mother that when Jim turned 18 years old, they were going to get him in the army. Jim agreed and was willing to join the army. Daddy and Mama had many sleepless nights worrying about their son. Sometimes Daddy stayed late working up town because Jim was around in the area. He wanted to make sure Jim didn't get into any trouble. Before Daddy would come home, he made sure Jim came home with him or that he was all right.

In 1960, we moved from Mr. George Brook's place to Mr. Tommie Heron's place. Mr. Tommy Heron was a well-known black businessman in Mound Bayou. My daddy and Mr.

Tommy Heron were very close and worked together with the NAACP to get people to register to vote. We chopped and picked cotton for Mr. Tommy Heron. He had all his children out there picking and chopping cotton.

My mother had many friends in Mound Bayou. Some names I remember and some I don't. I remember the Shannon family, the Bell family, and the Ross family. Whenever there was a need, they all worked together.

Mound Bayou was a nice place. We liked living there. There wasn't much crime there. When he lived there, Daddy was given a lot of respect by the people. He never had to arrest anyone. He was a police there.

We didn't know too much about Daddy. He was a quiet person and didn't talk a lot. He didn't have many friends. He never fought my mama, and I never heard them argue around us. They always went places together, and I followed them sometime. One time I watched Daddy play a piano. I loved my daddy. He was a good person. He made sure we had food on the table and clothes on our backs. We didn't have much.

Mound Bayou had few businesses that were black owned. The businesses were as follows: grocery stores, barber and beauty shops, clothes stores, service stations, night clubs, a funeral home, and a credit union. Mrs. Broomfield owned a night club. She was well respected. She loved everybody and had two children. Her club was located across the railroad track. As a matter of fact, the building is still standing now. Mr. Jack Bell and his wife had their own business, a club next to Mrs. Broomfield. The Bells were nice people and got along well with Daddy and other people. My father helped out in both clubs by making sure there was no fighting in either place.

When Jim turned 18 years old, Mama and Daddy took him down to join the army. Jim was willing to go to the army. But he didn't get the chance because he failed the test. Mama and Daddy were hurt because he didn't get into the army.

Jim was constantly provoked to fight by other young men. The kept messing with him. He had a fight with the Coleman boys. Jim went to jail a few times in Mound Bayou because of fighting, and Daddy got him out. A couple of times he broke out.

C.J. recalled one weekend night when they were at Mrs. Broomfield's club. Jim was having fun dancing and talking to other people when he was provoked. The place was crowded and everyone was having fun. Then a guy walked into the club from another town. He spotted Jim and deliberately stepped on Jim's shoes as he passed by. He refused to apologize. At that point in time, Jim knew that the guy was trying to pick a fight with him. He walked up to the guy and said something to him about stepping on his shoes. The guy said something smart, and Jim hit the guy and knocked him down to the floor.

Then the trouble began. People got up from their table and started running out of the place, ducking and hiding. C.J. said that Jim came out of his pocket with two guns and fired both in that place. Everybody was running and getting out of the way. The bullets went into the walls.

C.J. and Jim left the place before the Mound Bayou police got there. They split up as they went home. C.J. went over to Peewee's house. Jim came home wet and muddy because he walked across a muddy ditch in the back of the house. Mama asked him about his muddy shoes and wet appearance. He told her he got into trouble. He walked across the muddy ditch while he was running from the police. They were after him because he had shot up Mrs. Broomfield's place. He told her that C.J. was with him and that nobody got hurt. Mama questioned him about his father's whereabouts. He told her Daddy wasn't around when he got into the fight with the guy who stepped on his shoes and did not apologize to him. When he had finished telling Mama about the incident, he went into the room to change clothes and go to bed.

Daddy got the news and came home to see if Jim was all right. Daddy woke Jim up and told him the police were looking for him because Chief Byrd called the highway patrol, and it was a possibility that he might go to jail. Daddy told Jim not to go back to Mrs. Broomfield's place until everything cooled off.

The next morning Jim went back to Mrs. Broomfield's place to apologize to her about what he had done. While he was talking to Mrs. Broomfield, the Mound Bayou Chief of Police Byrd Isomer and Officer Ezell Anderson showed up. They wanted to take Jim to jail. Officer Ezell walked up to Jim, and Jim pushed him up off him, which caused the cigar to fall from the officer's mouth. Jim told Officer Ezell that he wasn't going to jail and to get back off of him. Both officers were afraid of Jim. Chief Byrd Isomer didn't say a word because he didn't want to mess with him. The two already did not get along. Jim refused to get in the patrol car, and Daddy came up to make Jim cooperate with the police. He did this because he knew Jim would go off on them. Jim stayed in police custody until the patrolman from Cleveland, Mississippi, came and took him away. He was sentenced and went to the reform school for a couple of months.

Jim loved to fight when he had to and would help his friends when they needed his help. He did not need anybody's help when he was fighting. Jim never picked a fight or cursed at anybody. He enjoyed sports: baseball, football, and boxing. Sometimes he wrestled with his friends because they wanted to see if they could handle him. He had a good relationship with his sister and brothers.

While he was locked up in the reform school, we went to see him and he told us that he had gotten into a fight with an inmate. The person started the fight by lying about him. He accused him about something he didn't do. The person kept picking on him. Jim didn't want to fight, but the person didn't leave him alone. Every time the guy saw Jim, he would tell him that he had heard about his reputation in the streets and how tough he was. Jim didn't like the guy's remarks. He hit that guy and knocked him down. He was out for a few minutes with blood running from his nose. The guy never bothered him again while he was there.

One day as I walked from up town on my way home, I saw a prison truck. As I got closer, prisoners were getting off the truck to work. They were not too far from our house. I heard someone call my name and wave at me to come closer. When I got a little closer, I recognized my brother. I walked up to him, and he let the others know that I was his little sister. Jim asked me about the rest of the family and how they were doing.

He hugged me and whispered in my ear to deliver a message to Mama. He told me to tell Mama he needed a few dollars. I ran home and told Mama that I had seen Jim and that he needed a few dollars. She came out on the porch and looked down the road in the direction where the prisoners were working. She was very happy. She gave me a $20.00 dollar bill to give to him. I rushed back to him and slipped the money into his hand without anyone seeing me. He hugged me again.

Then Jim said that he wanted to show me something and to stand back. I stood back and watched him pick up a big round heavy sewer pipe by himself and place it over in the ditch. The other prisoners stood back and watched him also. They did not believe it, and had no idea that Jim was going to do it. None of us knew that Jim was that strong. He looked at me and told me not to tell anyone. I ran home and told Mama what I had seen Jim do. After that incident, I kept his amazing strength a secret because I knew no one would believe me.

When Jim was released from reform school, his mind was made up. He wanted to stay out of trouble and not to go back to jail. He wanted to leave town and get a job in order to help take care of the family. He went back to picking cotton because he did not have any money.

Another time Jim showed off his strength was when Daddy had a flat tire while transporting cotton pickers to the cotton field. One morning Daddy's truck had a flat tire. Everybody got off the truck until the flat tire was changed. Daddy just couldn't get the jack to work. It really wasn't any good. So, Jim went behind the truck and picked it up until Daddy changed the flat. People were standing back and looking. I heard them talking among themselves about the amazing strength Jim had. Joe wanted to help hold the truck up, but Jim motioned for him to stay back.

I never did tell anyone about Jim's strength because I did not know what to say. I told Mama, and she said that she knew about it. C.J. knew, and other friends knew about his strength. Somebody questioned Daddy about his son's strength. Daddy didn't tell them anything because he really didn't know what was going on with his son. If he had known, he would have told anyone about his son.

Jim loved his family. He loved telling jokes and laughing with people. He won money from some guys. They bet him that he couldn't pick up a heavy weight, and he won their money.

One night there was a fight between Joe and another guy named Butch. It took place in front of Mrs. Crowder's grocery store. The young man was getting the best of Joe. Joe's friend, Arthur Home, ran and got Jim from across the track. He was at Mrs. Broomfield's cafe and told him that someone was jumping on his brother. Butch was down on Joe when Jim arrived with his friends, Frank Jr., June Lane, Hawk, and O.J Nelson. Jim walked up and pulled the guy up off of Joe. He then picked the guy up and threw him to the ground. Frank Jr., June Lane, and Hawk had to pull Jim off the young man. Jim told the guy to stay away from his brother. Jim and his friends went back to the café. The young man, Butch, had Jim arrested by the Mound Bayou police. They went to the café and arrested him. Joe stood around to see what they were going to do with his brother. Joe went home and told Daddy that Jim had gone to jail. Daddy left the house. He went and got his son from that jail. Jim didn't have any juvenile records.

Mound Bayou had a small jail. It was easy to break out of. One night Jim went to jail and Joe helped him to break out. The only time Jim went to jail was for fighting. I remember Jim jump on Norman. He owned a drug store in Mound Bayou. Dorothy went into Mr. Norman's drug store to buy herself something, and she picked up a watch. She got caught and told Mr. Norman that Jim told her to steal it, and Jim didn't know nothing about it. Mr. Norman got hold of Daddy and told him. Daddy went to Jim and questioned him. When Jim got away from Daddy, he went to Mr. Norman's drug store and confronted him about what Dorothy said. He jumped on Mr. Norman for lying on him. Daddy got on Jim about messing with that man.

One day C.J. said that Jim and his friends were at Mrs. Broomfield's café. They were sitting outside laughing, talking, and playing cards. Some guy from another town pulled up and started talking mess. Jim and his friends didn't know the person. The person continued to talk mess. So, Jim got up from his chair and went over to pull the person from his car. He hit the guy so fast and quick that the guy fell to the ground. He started kicking the person, and then he gradually picked him up over his head and threw him to ground. The person jumped up, got into his car, and took off. He was never seen again.

One weekend Jim went to a night club in Cleveland, Mississippi. Jim's friend June Lane and his sister U.Z. accompanied him. C.J. did not go with him that night because he was too young to go inside that place. Jim told C.J. while they were in the club, Jim saw a guy pulling on his friend's sister. She didn't want to dance with him. Jim walked over to the guy and told him to leave her alone. The guy started tough to Jim. So Jim hit the guy, and he fell back and hit the floor. All of sudden, five more guys started coming toward him. Jim and June Lane had to fight their way out of the club that night. Jim ended up whipping all five himself. He told Daddy that he didn't have any help.

They left there in a hurry and headed back to Mound Bayou. They next day those five people came to Mound Bayou looking for Jim and June Lane. Jim and June Lane showed up and faced the five young men. Whatever Jim said to those young men, they jumped in their cars and drove off.

Joe recalled one time when he and Jim walked to Shelby to shop for clothing. As Jim walked around the store, a man thought he was stealing something. He asked them to leave his store. Jim told the man they were looking for something to wear. The man threatened to call the police. They finally left. While they were walking, they got into somebody's parked car that had been left running. Jim and Joe left in the car. As Jim drove, he looked in his rearview mirror and saw the police coming behind them. He told Joe to hold on because he was going to ditch the police, and they did. While he was driving fast, he crossed the railroad track and the car went out of control. It turned over in a ditch. They got out and ran down into a cotton field. They walked home without any injury, but they were a little dazzled. The police never found out who was driving the car.

One day across the track at Mrs. Broomfield café, Jim and others were playing games. Some guy was cheating, and Jim caught him cheating. The guy got smart, and Jim jumped up, hit the guy in his mouth, and knock him down to the floor. T.J. jumped up and started taking up for the young man. Jim told T.J. to stay out of it and threw him to the ground. Jim wanted to shoot him, but Mrs. Broomfield and others told him not to. Someone called the police. And when Ezell Anderson and Chief Byrd Isomer drove up, they wanted to arrest him. The police tried to put the handcuff on Jim, but they couldn't bring his hands together. Jim kept pulling his hands apart. Someone went and got Daddy. People in the back were laughing and talking, and Jim was smiling because they couldn't arrest him. Daddy walked up and told them let him handle his son. Jim didn't go to jail that time.

Another time, Daddy went to Cleveland to see Mr. Amzie Moore on business. Jim asked Mama if he could use Daddy's truck to go somewhere, and he asked me to go with him. Riding around town and driving fast out in the county, I was afraid he was going to have an accident. One time he took his eye off the road to see who was calling him, and he almost ran off the road into a ditch. I told him take me back home before Daddy made it back. Daddy found out Jim had his truck. He fussed at Jim about driving his truck.

One night Daddy was sitting in his chair sleeping. I walked over to the window to look out of it and saw Daddy's truck moving from the yard. I saw two people pushing the truck away from the yard. I woke Daddy up and told him that someone was trying to steal his truck. Daddy jumped up from his chair and got his gun. He went outside and fired a shot. The two ran down the cotton field. Daddy pulled his truck back into the yard. He never did find out who was trying to steal his truck.

One night in November of 1961, it was pouring down rain. Mama was having labor pains. She sent Joe to go and get Daddy. Daddy was up town across the tract, over in Mr. Jack Bell's café. Daddy owned a 1957 green Ford truck, which Mama gave him the keys to. Joe, Earnest, and Arthur Holmes left together. Arthur Holmes was Joe's friend. They stayed up town until it stopped raining. Joe did not go into the café because of his age, so he sent Arthur Holmes in to get Daddy. Daddy came out, and Joe told Daddy that Mama was not feeling good. Daddy told Joe to tell Mama he'd be right on, and he told Joe to take his truck back home and give the keys back to Mama. Daddy very seldom drove his truck unless he was going to another town.

After the heavy rain stopped, Joe started home and had an accident with a car. Joe told Earnest to go home and tell Mama about the accident. Arthur Holmes was told by Joe to go and report the accident to Daddy. When Earnest came home, he told Mama about the accident in Daddy's truck and that he and Joe were all right.

Mama told me and Earnest to go back and see about Joe. When we walked back to the accident, we saw Joe sitting in the man's car in the back seat, along with the man and his wife. I walked up to the car and asked Joe if he was all right. Then Joe told me that the man hit him up side his face and made him get into his car. I told Joe that he needed to get out of the man's car, and he refused because the man wouldn't let him out. I stood there talking to Joe, and I looked around and up the road and saw Jim and Frank Jr. They were alerted by Arthur Holmes, who ran into them before he had contacted Daddy.

When Jim and Frank walked up to the man's car and asked Joe what was going on, Joe told Jim that the man ran into them. He also told Jim that the man hit him up side his face and made him get into his car. Jim told Joe to get out of the man's car. The man was standing in front of his car. Jim walked over to the man and asked if he had struck his brother. The man denied it and told Jim that Joe ran into him. The man got smart with Jim, and he hit the man so fast and quick in the face that the man fell to the ground out cold. He started kicking the man. Frank Jr. tried to pull Jim off the man, but Jim told him to get back.

The man's woman pleaded for Jim to leave him alone. I was hoping and wishing someone would break the fight up. I looked up and saw Daddy and Arthur Holmes walking together. Daddy walked up and made Jim leave the man alone. Jim did what Daddy told him to do.

A few minutes later, Police Officer Ezell drove up and helped Daddy pick the man up off the ground. They put him back in his car, and Daddy told the woman to take him to the nearby hospital. Daddy wanted Joe to explain what had happened. Joe told Daddy that on his way, the guy ran into him because he was hugged up with his woman. Ezell Anderson asked Jim why he hit the man. Jim told Ezell the man hit his brother and cursed at him. Ezell wanted to arrest Jim for jumping on the man. Jim told Ezell Anderson that he wasn't going to jail, and he told Ezell to get out of his face. Jim pointed his finger at him and repeated again what he said. Jim was determined that he wasn't going to jail but home that night. Jim kept telling Ezell Anderson over and over again that he wasn't going to jail.

Jim walked back up to Ezell Anderson, and Ezell Anderson reached for his gun. Daddy told Ezell Anderson that if he shot his son, he was going to be in a world of trouble and to put his gun down. At that point, Jim backed away from Ezell Anderson and started walking toward home, telling Ezell Anderson that he wasn't going to jail but home that night. Jim walked a couple of feet and turned around, still telling Ezell Anderson to shoot.

Jim kept pointing his finger at Ezell Anderson and telling him to shoot. Daddy finally got Jim to calm down. Daddy told Jim to come back, and Jim told Daddy that he wasn't going to jail. Daddy told Jim to shut up and let him handle it. But for now they needed to straighten things out between the man and Joe. Frank Jr., Joe, Jim, and Daddy got in the police man's car. Daddy told Earnest and I to go home as he instructed.

As they drove away, I asked Earnest go give me the keys to the truck. He didn't want to give them to me. I told him that I was going to tell Daddy. He gave up the keys, and I drove the truck back home. That was my first time under a steering wheel with C.J.'s help. I learned how to drive a little from C.J., who taught me from time to time. We came home and told Mama what had happened. She was a little upset and worried about Jim getting himself into trouble.

Jim didn't go to jail that night, although Ezell Anderson and Police Chief Byrd wanted to call the highway patrol to arrest Jim. But Daddy wanted them to drop the charged on Jim. Daddy paid a fine to keep Jim out of jail. Daddy didn't trust Ezell and Chief Byrd.

Daddy knew that Mr. John Wise was leaving town that night, taking people down to Miami, Florida. Daddy went to him and told him that his son was in trouble with the police. He asked if Jim could go to Florida with him. He told Daddy that he would be leaving around midnight.

Daddy, Jim, Joe, and Arthur Holmes came. Daddy told Mama he had to get Jim out of town before he went to jail. Jim started packing his clothes. Jim knew he was in trouble with the police. Near midnight, they knew it was time for them to leave the house. Jim hugged me and the rest of us. I didn't want to see my brother go. Mama, Grandmother, Joe, and Arthur Holmes all left with Daddy to meet Mr. John Wise up town. C.J. was already up town and waiting to see his brother to get on the truck. They met up with Mr. John Wise near the hospital in Mound Bayou.

Jim got on the truck without the police seeing him. He knew all the people on the truck. They heard about what had happened, and they were happy that he was going for the ride. A few minutes later, the highway patrol showed up looking for Jim. They talked to Mr. John Wise and wanted to search his truck to see if Jim was among the people. Jim was hiding behind the people, and they were not asked to get off the truck. They did not recognize him among the people because they didn't see him. Ezell and Chief Byrd did not see him either. The highway patrol did not hang around too long and soon left.

Daddy told Mr. John Wise he would meet up with him outside of Merry Go, Mississippi, to make sure nobody was following them. John Wise stopped his truck on the way and waited for Daddy. He told Daddy that the police were following him. The police drove a few miles and turned around. Jim got off the truck, hugged Daddy, Mama, Grandmother, Joe, and Arthur, and told them to take care of themselves. He would be in touch when he got up on his feet and landed a job. He got back up on the truck and waved goodbye to them. They pulled off. Daddy turned his truck around and headed back home.

When they made it to Florida, John Wise got in touch with Daddy. He let him know that Jim was all right. He was staying at his friend's house. That person's name was Memes.

Two week later, Mama gave birth to a little girl and she named her Martha. Jim kept in touched with us for a while, but we didn't hear from him for a long time.

Somebody told Daddy that Jim got into a little trouble in Miami while he was living there. He had to leave that town. Daddy was told that he had cut two people because they were trying to kill his friend. He was in a café sitting around, and someone told him that people were trying to kill his friend. Jim rushed outside, and someone was trying to run over the guy with their car. Jim ran and pulled the guy out of his car, pulled out his razor, and cut the lip off. The guy's friend jumped on Jim, and Jim took his razor and cut the guy's ears off. As they fought, Jim's hand got cut. He lost a lot of blood. In the struggle, Jim had to fight his way out of trouble. He left there running and ran into the police. They tried to arrest him. He had to fight with them because they were beating him with their sticks. He got away and ran. He went to the hospital because he lost of blood. They never did catch up with him because they didn't have any lead without a picture of him.

He wrote and told Mama and Daddy that he got into a little trouble and was leaving Florida. They didn't hear from him again. While he was still in Florida, he was caught with an aggravated assault charge in 1962. His court record said on April 5, 1963, in Dade County, Florida, he went to jail for using a deadly weapon. Jim plea admitted the offense because of an argument over some money that the victim owed him for working in the victim's café. The victim refused to give him any money and threatened to throw him out of the café if he didn't leave. The man put his hand in his pocket, and Jim thought he was getting a knife. So, Jim pulled out his knife and cut the guy several times on the arms. He fled the café and caught the bus. A short time later, the police stopped the bus and arrested him. He was put on probation and failed to report to his probation officer. Jim was arrested again on October 23, 1963, placed in the Dade County Jail, and remained in that jail until he was brought to the Florida State Courts. He was sentenced for two years. I have a copy of his court record. He never went to jail for killing or robbing people.

Jim wrote Daddy and told him what had happened, and then he didn't write for a while. Mama and Daddy went to see a woman in Clarkdale, Mississippi, concerning Jim's welfare. The woman told them that he was alright, but he was in a little trouble. She assured us that we would be hearing from him very soon. We got a letter from Jim saying he was alright and he would be coming home July 1, 1965. He wanted to know how the family was doing. I wrote Jim back and sent him my $2.00. He answered me back, and then he stopped writing for a while.

When he was locked up on April 4, 1964, the report stated that an inmate said that he had a gold ring and also one pair of sun shades missing from his locker. Later, this inmate Woodson was found to have the above mentioned shades. When he was questioned about the glasses and ring he lied. Jim said he had got the glasses from another inmate and he didn't know about a ring. However, when Woodson could not get anyone to lie for him, he told the truth and said that he had taken the glasses and the ring. He had never given the ring away. The ring was recovered also.

On May 3, 1964, the supervisor asked inmate Woodson what squad he was assigned to. Woodson replied that he was in the yard square. They checked his card. It showed he was assigned to farm squad. Woodson lied. Woodson's attitude was fair when he was confined.

On May 28, 1964, the offense was down on the east of dormitory when he heard a noise. He went west of the dormitory. He wanted to see what was going on, and he saw inmate Willie Woodson Jr. and inmate Leonard Cooper Jr. fighting. He broke it up once, and while he was holding Cooper, Woodson jumped on him again. Willie admitted the fight to him. He talked to other inmates about it. Inmate Leonard Cooper Jr. and Willie had an argument in the dormitory. Willie struck the first blow that started the fight. He did not stop fighting when ordered to do so by Officer Sheffey. Inmate Cooper was confined after admitting action by the Disciplinary Committee.

Jim carried a generically medium custody status when not in punishment. He was in isolation, having been placed there by reason of a disciplinary imposed on December 9, 1964. He was released, after being isolated for stealing and lying, on April 18, 1964. It was not his only time spent in isolation.

Woodson was assigned to duties on farm squad #1-12-13-63. There had been no change in job status, but he had several times asked for job changes, one being driving a tractor, but his difficulties of adjustment so far have mitigated against his receiving consideration by the classification committee.

The inmate was assigned to dormitory A quarters. He received one reprimand for leaving shorts in the shower room. There were a few disciplinary reports made on him while he was in there.

It was voting time. Daddy helped people in Mound Bayou and other local towns register to vote. Other local towns did the same. Daddy worked closely with Mr. Amie Moore, who represented the Cleveland, Mississippi field office. The people in Mound Bayou brought Dr. Martin Luther King Jr. in and out of Mound Bayou whenever he had to speak about voter registration. My daddy was one of the leaders in the civil rights movement in Mound Bayou.

As time move on, we had a lots of fun as children, playing with each other and other children. I can recall people got a long with each other, and I remember Daddy had a pet hog that had many baby piglets. Some of them were stolen and the remaining died. The hog was white and fat. We were crazy about her. She was a very friendly pet and would let anyone ride on her back. When she got tired of carrying us, she would pick up speed and throw us off her back. There were times when she would wonder off and return by late evening. Nobody bothered her.

Our grandmother's husband gave C.J. a dog. He didn't want the dog anymore. C.J. named her Whitly because her color was snow white. C.J. trained her to be very bad. We had to keep her tied up. The dog didn't want anyone near her but C.J. Sometimes she allowed us to get closer to her, but that was only because she was chained. We put all kinds of chains on her, but she would break them and run away and get behind people. We had to find her, and C.J. would have to tie her up again. We didn't want her to bite anyone. C.J. was the only one who could handle her. Sometimes she would break lose and chase people. We had to find C.J. in order for the dog to be tied properly.

One day Whitely broke her chain, and she went running after Daddy's hog and attacked her. She bit both of her ears off. The hog disappeared for two days. My brother and I went looking for her, but we couldn't find her. We thought someone had taken her or she was dead somewhere.

One night I was on my way home and heard something coming through the cotton field. I stopped in my tracks, became frozen in time, and was too afraid to move. I actually did not know what to do. My first choice was to run home. But if I ran home, then I would have to pass another house before I reached mine. But I was terrified of passing alone because it could have got me before I made it home. Then I had a second choice of turning around and going back up town to find Daddy. I chose neither and continued to walk. All of sudden, I saw a white head coming out of the cotton field.

I thought it was a bear with no ears, so I turned around and took off running as fast as I could. While I was running, I could still hear it coming behind me, making scary noises. I became more fearful. With all the uncertainty, I was just too afraid to look back to see what it was that was following me.

When I reached the highway, I tried to cross over, I saw a man standing in front of a store. I ran around him and held on to him, and when I looked back I did not realize that it was our hog. The hog scared the man, but I told him it was our hog. I took the hog back home because she was following me.

One night C.J. was coming home, and something came up behind him out of the cotton field making noise. He didn't look back and took off running. He ran by the front door of the house and headed toward the back. He ran into a clothes line he didn't see. He couldn't go any further. He really didn't know what else to do until he saw the hog following him. That hog scared a lot of people.

There were a lot of crazy things going on around that house. One night while Mama and Daddy were gone, we would hear something jumping up and down on the porch, making some kind of noise as it blew its breath into the keyhole. We all sat still, waiting until Daddy came home and told him about it. Daddy stayed home one night with his gun beside him and nothing happened. We told C.J. about it, and he stayed home with us. He also heard the noise. He got up and removed Daddy's rifle from the wall, and he shot outside. After that, it never happened again.

Another night while I was in bed, I saw a man with a hat on his head pass by my window, but he kept walking toward the back of the house. We told Daddy everything that went on. Daddy told C.J. to stay closer to the house when he was not around. Mama and Grandmother were there most of the time, and they heard something.

One night in 1963, Daddy was sitting in his chair and fell asleep. I came in the living room and looked out the window and saw someone pushing daddy's truck out of the yard. I woke him up. Daddy got up and removed his rifle from the wall, and he shot outside. They ran away.

Sometimes when it rained, Daddy would leave his truck near the gravel road because he didn't want to get stuck in the mud coming home.

Another time I remember Daddy coming home and falling asleep in his chair. I looked out the window and saw that his truck was on fire! I saw two people near the truck. I woke Daddy up and told him that his truck was on fire. He jumped up, taking his gun and going down the road to see who it was, but he saw no one. The truck was burned up.

The next day, he went to report the burned up truck to the police. They didn't believe him. They wanted to give him a hard time about his truck. They wanted to charge him for something he did not do. I am a witness to that. I actually saw someone at his truck that night.

Daddy had to go to court. He took C.J. and Joe as witnesses. He was found guilty of burning his own truck up. Joe told Mama and me that the police officer made him say that Daddy burned his own truck while they forced a gun up his nose. He said that he was afraid and testified against his own father. C.J. did not have much to say because he wasn't around to see anything.

Daddy went to jail too after Jim was sentenced and locked up. Daddy was sentenced from 1963 to 1964. He stayed in prison about a year. While he was in there, he went blind in both eyes. We went to visit Daddy every chance we got. The Lord blessed him to see again.

I don't remember what caused him to go blind, and I never knew why. Mama had to take care of the family. It was hard on her because Daddy was not around to help. Joe, Earnest, and I, we had go out pick and chop cotton to help out.

When Joe turned eighteen years old on September 16, 1963, he wanted to leave home. Daddy told him that he should stay with the family until he was released from that place. However, Joe did not want to wait. He went to the cotton field and made himself some money. He told Mama that he wanted to go and find Jim because he was worried about him. Mama tried to talk to him out of going, but his mind was made up. One day Joe left us. Joe left us in the early part of November.

My grandmother had to help with the family. Joe wrote me a few letters to let us know how he was and where he was staying. He lived at one time in the states of New York and Virginia.

We moved from Mr. Tommy Heron's place because it was raining in the house. We moved into one of Mrs. Johnson's houses. She was a very nice woman and close to the family. She also worked with the civil rights moment. She owned a grocery store. She let people have food on credit.

We left our hog behind. Me and my brothers wanted her to have a place to live. Sometimes we would go back to check on her every day. One day we went back to check on her, and we couldn't find her. We kept on looking for her. When we found her near the ditch in the back of the house, we noticed something was wrong with one of her legs. We doctored her legs and fed her hog food. When we went back another time to check on her and found her dead. It hurt the family so much because she was a good hog and very friendly.

One night our mother was gone and left our grandmother in charge. She spent the night with us. Grandmother wanted something from the store. She sent Earnest, Dean, T.W., and Jessie to the store and ordered them to go and come right back. They were known for horsing around. As they approached the front door, Dean went out first and saw something with big red eyes. It blew its hot breath in their faces. It happened so fast and quick. They all took off running just like a flash of lighting toward the back with grandmother and the rest of us right behind. We hid in the closet, leaving the front door wide open. We were too afraid to come out to see what it was that frightened us. We were terrified of closing the front door. My grandmother told me to go and shut the door. I finally came out of the closet, ran up to the front door of the house, and shut the door. We all came out the closet and went back into the living room. We never found out what it was that scared us so badly. I found later that my brother Dean was known for seeing things. We told Mama what had happen when she came home.

One morning something else happened. My mother left the house to go and get us some food. Earnest put on Mama's coat and stood by the fireplace to keep warm. I told him that he needed to back away from the fireplace before he caught on fire. He refused because he said that he wanted to stay warm. It was cold outside during the month of December in 1963. Within minutes, the housecoat caught on fire because his back was turned to the fire. He began dancing around the room on fire and ran into the other bedroom where C.J. was. C.J. jumped out of bed, ran for water, and threw it on him. The housecoat was stuck to his body. Mama came home and had to take him to the nearby hospital in Mound Bayou. He was burnt very badly and couldn't sit down at all. He had blisters on his butt and thighs. When he tried to sit down, he was in pain. He walked funny like a duck, and we had fun laughing at him. Mama took care of him until he got better. He still has scars on him to this very day.

In the early part of 1964, Daddy was released from prison and came to the house. He got himself together and built a home for is family. Around April of 1964, we moved into our new home. My mother left us and went to Memphis, Tennessee to help her cousin Earnestine take of her mother. I had to learn how to cook for the kids, and I sent them to school while Daddy was at work.

Later on I received a letter from Joe, who was living in Virginia. He wanted me to tell Daddy to send him fifty dollars so he could come home. Daddy was still angry with him because he had left home when he was asked to stay with the family. Daddy told me that he was not going to send him anything. I wrote and told Joe what Daddy had said. The last time I got a letter from him, he was on his way to Miami to visit Jim. After that I stopped getting letters from him.

I called Mama every day, and she said she would be home very soon. Daddy knew Jim would be coming home very soon, and he didn't want to live in Mound Bayou anymore. Jim wrote Daddy when he was getting out soon. While Jim was locked up and soon to be released, Daddy made up his mind to leave Mound Bayou because of Jim.

Daddy had heard rumors of what the police said about his son. They said that if that Woodson boy ever came back to Mound Bayou, they were going to get him. Daddy spoke about the rumor, saying that nobody was going to hurt his son and if they did they would have to hurt him also. He really didn't want Jim to get into any more trouble, nor did he want him back in town.

Daddy and I talked about many things. Some things were about Jim. Daddy told me that he was going to find a way to take care of us, and that one day we all were going to miss him. We talked about many things, but I don't remember them all. Mama was pregnant at the time, and Daddy said that she would be home soon. While he was talking to me about Jim, tears came to his eyes. He was worried about Jim and Mama. When he was finished talking to me about Jim and moving out of town, he told me to go and get C.J., that he needed to talk to him.

One my way to deliver Daddy's message to C.J., I passed by a store and saw a newspaper article about a prize fight. I picked it up and saw Jim and another person's picture. They were being featured as prize fighters. The event was to be held on May 30, 1965, the exact day we had planned to move.

I continued on over to where C.J. was, over at his friend Pee Wee's house. I showed him the newspaper and told him Daddy wanted to talk to him. He told me to tell Daddy that I had seen him. C.J. told me he was not moving to Jackson, Mississippi.

I returned home and showed Daddy the newspaper about the fight. Daddy asked me if I delivered the message. I told him I left the message to give to C.J. because C.J. was not there.

In preparing to move, I asked Daddy if I could remain and stay with Grandmother for a while and watch the fight. I was told no because he needed me to help with the younger sisters and brothers until Mama came back home. Sometime after that, even C.J. came home and talked to Daddy. He wanted C.J. to come along, and C.J. promised Daddy he would. And Daddy asked C.J. to stay around the house until he got back. He had to go to Jackson to borrow a truck from someone. Daddy left the next day in his truck. While Daddy was gone, C.J. told me he was not moving with us and he told me not to tell Daddy. He stayed until Daddy came home. Daddy asked him to come back later on to help load the truck for moving.

C.J. gave his word and said he would return to help load the truck. He told me he had a feeling that Daddy might talk him into coming along. He never showed up. Daddy already had a place for us to stay.

Before midnight, we started loading everything on the truck. We didn't take everything, only clothes and little furniture. We had to help Daddy pack our things. Daddy waited for a few minutes on C.J., and I told Daddy he was not coming with us.

Around midnight, we pulled out of town without anybody noticing us. On our way to Clinton, Mississippi, we stopped in Shaw to see Uncle Jeff, the man Daddy called his brother. I don't know if he was Daddy's brother or not. I believe they were very close friends. He told us once that he was his half-brother. Daddy let Uncle Jeff know where he was moving in Clinton, Mississippi.

When we made it to our new home, it was already furnished. Daddy had the house looking nice. It was a three-bedroom house with a kitchen and dinner room. Daddy had everything we needed.

People's houses were so far apart from each other. And the store was two miles from where we lived. Next morning before he went to work, he gave me money to buy food. We had to walk two miles to get to the store.

Also, there were no other children to play with. Daddy knew we were unhappy, but he was doing this for Jim. I had to cook for the family. I learned to cook before we left Mound Bayou.

Dorothy and I got together and talked. We were going to ask Daddy if we could go back to Mound Bayou to live with Grandmother. We were afraid to ask him because we knew what he was going to say. I told Dorothy I would talk to Daddy when he came home from work.

One day when he came home from work, I went to him and said I wanted to go back to Mound Bayou and live with Grandmother because I didn't like it here. He told me to wait until the Fourth of July because Mama and Jim were coming and we were going over to our cousin's house to play with their children. Daddy wasn't so happy himself. He was so tired when he come from work.

When that weekend came, we went over to our cousin's house and played with their children and rode their horse. On our way back home we stopped in Jackson. Daddy wanted us to meet our Grandfather, my mother's daddy, but he wasn't home. After that, I didn't bother him anymore about leaving. I began to realize he really needed me and Dorothy around the house to cook and clean. I told Dorothy I was not going to ask Daddy anymore about leaving.

When Daddy went to work, we went and picked blueberries. I would come home and make a blueberry pie for dinner for the family. Daddy loved it, and it became his favorite dish.

We didn't have a television to watch. It was boring to us with no one to play because no children were around to play with. We played with each other.

On June 10, 1965, Daddy came home from work, ate, took a bath, and sat down with us for a while. He fell asleep while sitting in his rocking chair in front of the fireplace. I was the only one awake. Everyone else was asleep. Daddy woke up and came in our room to check on us. He told me he would see me in the morning.

I went to bed and fell asleep. Dorothy was in her bed next to mine asleep. Some time around two in the morning, I heard Dorothy calling my name. Mary, Mary. She wanted me to get up. She had woken up and found Daddy dead. I thought she was playing and told her to leave me alone. I finally got up and went into his room to see if she was telling the truth or not. I shook Daddy a few times and called him. He did not answer. I touched his face and it was still warm. Dorothy told me that Daddy was calling my name, and she went to see what was wrong. He was still warm and lying there, not moving.

Then I started crying. I woke everybody up and told them that Daddy was dead. Everybody started crying. We did not have a telephone in the house to make a call. The man Daddy worked for stayed back down in the woods. It was very dark and we were afraid to go to get him during those early hours in the morning. So, Daddy laid there until five in the morning.

Earnest and I walked down into the wood to get to Daddy's boss man's house. We stood there almost thirty minutes calling their names, him and his wife. Their dog was barking and we were afraid to get any closer to their house. They finally came to the window, and we told them that Daddy was dead. They came right over. They called for an ambulance and let the police know what was going on.

The police questioned Dorothy and me about Daddy's death. I told them I didn't know what happened to Daddy and I was asleep when Dorothy woke me up to tell me Daddy was dead. They questioned Dorothy, and I don't remember what she told them. When they got through questioning us, they wanted to know if we had any other place to go. The police took us over to our cousin's. I used their phone and called Mama and C.J. I told them the bad news.

Mama caught the bus to Mound Bayou and picked up Grandmother. They rode the bus together and came right on down to Clinton. Everybody who heard the shocking news in Mound Bayou it took very hard. At the funeral, we all took it very hard. My mother fainted twice at the funeral, but my cousin O.W. Steward caught her before she hit the floor. My daddy's sister took it hard. The other sister was ill and could not attend the funeral. Daddy's sister, our Aunt Polly, fainted twice at the funeral. I could not stand to see him lying there in the casket. C.J. did not attend the service because he did not want to see Daddy in that casket.

At the burial, my mother fainted again. At the grave site ceremony, Daddy's sister wanted to see her brother one more time. When they opened the casket, I ran from the grave back to the car and watched. With tears in my eyes, I looked as they rolled Daddy down into the grave.

We stayed in Clinton for a week after the funeral. We left all our belongings behind because we couldn't bring them back on the Greyhound bus. And most of all, we left our Daddy behind, but his memory stayed in our hearts. My little brother Jessie and my sister Dorothy wanted to stay for the summer until school started. Mama let them stay a little longer.

When we returned to Mound Bayou we lived with our grandmother. She had a two-room house. The reason we couldn't go back to our old house was because Daddy had sold it to someone.

Mama knew Jim was coming home soon. She didn't to write to let him know about Daddy's death because she thought he might do something crazy, like break out of jail.

On July 1, 1965, he was released from the Florida State Prison. He arrived in Mound Bayou on July, 2, 1965. When he got off the Greyhound bus, he didn't know which way to go because it wasn't the same. He started walking toward the post office because he didn't know where we lived. Earnest had a part time job cleaning up around the post office. He looked up and saw Jim walking toward him. He dropped whatever he had in his hands and ran to Jim. They hugged each other. Jim asked about the family and wanted to know where we were. Earnest told him that everybody was doing fine. Jim asked about Daddy, and Earnest told him he didn't know where Daddy was. Jim wanted to know where C.J. was. Earnest told him that he was over at Pee Wee's house. Jim walked away and Earnest went back to work.

When Jim made it over to Mr. Frank's house, somebody saw him walking down the street and alerted C.J. that his brother was in town. C.J. walked out on the porch and saw Jim coming toward him. He called out his name and told him that he didn't know he was coming home. They hugged each other and went into the house. Pee Wee and his brothers were happy to see him also. Jim sat down and talked with them for a while. Jim found out that C.J. was living with Mr. Frank and his sons.

Soon he got up and told C.J. to take him to visit the rest of the family. He wanted to see Mama, his little sisters and brothers, and Daddy. While they were walking, he asked C.J. about Daddy. C.J. hesitated for a few minutes. Jim became annoyed and asked again about Daddy. C.J. saw that Jim was getting angry and told him that Daddy was dead. Tears started coming down his eyes. Jim wanted to know how long Daddy had been dead. He was told since last month in June of 1965. Then Jim wanted to know what happened. He was told he died in his sleep. He wanted to know why he wasn't notified and about his father's death. C.J. told him the family didn't know his address and didn't know where he was. At that point, he had very little to say.

When the moment of silence was over, he told C.J. that he was glad to see him and it was good to be home.

They walked over to Grandmother's house. I was not there at this time. When they got there, C.J. told Jim to hide beside the house in order to surprise the whole family. C.J. walked into the house and sat down for a few minutes. Suddenly Jim walked in and Mama and Grandmother jumped up and ran to him. He was happy to see them. He was hiding behind the door when I walked into the house. He grabbed me from behind and picked me up. I didn't know what to expect, and I looked back in his face and saw who he was. We all sat down and talked.

I could tell something was on his mind because he had a frown on his face. He told us he saw Joe in Florida, standing on a street. He and another inmate were on the truck going back to the place. He called out his name, and Joe looked around and recognized it was Jim. Then Joe called Jim's name and they waved at each other. That was the last time they saw each other. Jim thought Joe would visit him in prison, but he didn't.

Still shocked over the news of Daddy's death later on, Jim questioned Mama about it. He wanted to know how long ago the death had occurred. All questions that came to his mind he asked. Mama tried to fill him in on everything he wanted to know. He wanted to know everything. He wanted to know what happened to Daddy and where he was buried. Mama told him that she got the news of his death while she was in Memphis seeing about her sick aunt. She told him where Daddy was buried.

Jim wanted to go and visit Daddy's grave site and also see his little brother and sister, who had remained there for the summer. He looked forward to seeing Dorothy and Jessie. He didn't have but a few dollars on him. So, I gave him my little savings I had saved up from picking cotton to help him get a round-trip ticket by bus to go and visit Daddy's grave. He told me that he was going to pay me back when he found himself a job.

The next morning he caught the Greyhound bus in Mound Bayou and went to Clinton. When he arrived, he went over to our cousin's house where Dorothy and Jessie were staying. He spent the night with them, and he didn't get a chance to visit Daddy's grave because it was too far out.

The next morning, he got up and asked Jessie and Dorothy if they were ready to go back home with him. Jessie said no. He said Jim picked him up and sat him on his lap, trying again to encourage him to go back home. So, Jim got up and said goodbye to everyone. Jessie said as Jim departed, he left walking, and he watched Jim until he got out of sight. Jim caught the next bus headed for Mound Bayou.

The following day, Jim spent time with family and friends. In the little time he had with Mama, he told her that he wanted to leave town, get a job, and help her and his little sisters and brothers. He didn't like the way we were living in a two-room house, and he wanted to take care of his family. He told Mama that he missed Daddy so much. Then Mama could tell something was bothering him. He tried to hide it because he didn't want Mama to worry about him.

C.J. came over, sat down, and talked with him for a while. Jim went back home with him. As they walked, he constantly mentioned how much he missed Daddy. He told C.J. that if Daddy was dead, he might as well be dead too. He talked as if he didn't want to live anymore because Daddy was the only person he could talk to. He expressed that he didn't like how the family was living and that they needed him around to help. He mentioned how necessary it was for him to find a job. He said that this was what Daddy wanted him to do. He said he knew Mama needed help with the younger children.

C.J. said Jim never looked at him while they were walking and talking. He noticed something was worrying him by the way he talked. He told Jim to get himself together and stop worrying about things. Jim wanted to tell C.J. something, but was afraid he would go back and tell Mama. C.J. tried to get Jim to talk to him. Jim never got a chance to tell C.J. what he wanted him to know.

Jim's friends welcomed him back to Mound Bayou. He visited Reverend Oral D. Robinson, one of his old friends. He was surprised Jim had come back home. Mr. Robinson was the pastor of his own church and a family marriage counselor.

Most of Jim's friends had moved away from Mound Bayou. So, he chatted with Mrs. Broomfield, and she told me that he told her that his daddy was dead and he might as well be dead too. She told him to pray and ask the Lord for help. Mrs. Broomfield told me that Jim sat down in front of her with tears coming down his face.

He sat down with the family and told us about the trouble he had gotten into while he was in Florida. He was found guilty of aggravated assault. He was working for this man, and he got involved in an argument over some money. The victim refused to give him any money and threatened to throw him out the café if he didn't leave. The man then put his hand in his pocket, and Jim pulled out his knife and cut the man several times on the arms.

He fled the café and caught a bus. A short time later, the city police stopped the bus and arrested him. He went to prison because he didn't report to his probate. He told us he whipped five police officers off him because they were beating him. He got away, and they never caught up with him. I don't remember all the details. He mentioned the time he went to prison, and while he was in lock up he got into a fight with a guy. They put him in a hole and fed him three beans a day and a little water. He experienced hunger and became very weak.

Then I remembered the picture in the newspaper about the prize fight and asked him about it. He told us that he changed his name because he did not want anyone to recognize him. He said he won the fight and didn't want to stay on the subject too long.

He told Mama he had made two wedding rings, one for the man and another for the woman. He made those rings while he was locked up. He told Mama to keep the rings until he found that woman. The woman he really cared about lived in Mound Bayou. He wanted to talk to her about their intimate relationship concerning marriage. I don't know what happened after that, and I don't know if he talked to her or not. I believe he did because Mama told me Jim told her he was going to get married.

One day, he got a letter from his friend June Lane, who lived in St. Louis, Missouri. June Lane told him that he would be down to pick him up in a few days. Jim told Mama that he was going to St. Louis with June Lane. He had gotten Jim a job. Jim wanted the job in order to help the family out because he didn't like the way we were living.

Another time, the family got together to enjoy each other, and Jim entertained us. He told jokes and showed us some of his tricks. For example, he told me to go get two bath towels. Earnest and I had a towel tied around our waists. Jim told us not to be afraid and that he was not going to hurt us. Slowly, he picked both of us up at the same time. He also showed us how he could knock a gun out of a police officer's hand. He told me he was not going to hurt me. He told me what to do. I took one of the children's guns and put it behind his back. He moved a couple of steps and turned so fast that he knocked the gun clean out of my hand. The gun went towards the ceiling. He wanted to show us more tricks, but he never got a chance.

One morning as Mama was cooking breakfast, Jim stood in the kitchen doorway. He inquired about if there was really a heaven and hell. Mama told him yes.

Then he wanted to know how she knew. She told him the Bible said so. He told her that he had a bad dream during the night. The dream was about C.J., and he was lying in a pool of blood. Jim took him to the hospital. He asked Mama about the meaning of the dream. She told him she didn't know right then. Mama told me she began to wonder about the peculiar question he was asking. Then he asked another question. He wanted to know how old he was. She told him he was 22 years old. She thought it was unusual and strange that he had forgotten his age. And she didn't understand why he had asked her so many questions. Mama knew something was wrong.

At the dinner table, he told her how much he missed Daddy. Mama told him that the whole family missed him. Mama told him not to get in trouble. He told Mama he was not going back to jail because he was trying to get his life back together. Mama was between six or eight months pregnant.

Mama and grandmother gave him some money to buy some clothes. He only had a couple pairs of pants when he came home. He caught the bus and went to Cleveland to buy some clothes. On his way back home, he saw a parked car that was left running. He got into the car and drove himself back home. He parked the car two blocks away from the house until it was found. Nobody knew he had taken the car and driven it home.

Whatever he had done, he tried not to hide it from Mama. She knew her son well. She also knew something was troubling him. Once I overheard Mama and Grandmother talking about Jim. They were saying that death must be on him and he didn't know how to handle it. He was trying to hide it.

One day, Jim saw Daddy's shot gun inside of Grandmother's chifforobe where she kept her clothes and personal things. He took Daddy's shotgun and sawed it down to half its size.

Every time he would leave the house, he would carry the gun with him for protection. He didn't trust anyone because he knew there were people who didn't like him. He went to visit C.J. and they went for a walk. C.J. noticed how Jim was walking and asked if anything was wrong with his leg. Jim told him that he had a gun down inside his pants. C.J. asked him about the purpose of the gun. He was told it was for protection only. Jim expressed that he didn't trust people. C.J. reminded him not to get into any more trouble. C.J. became a little nervous. He knew how his brother was. He also knew that if anyone messed with Jim or him trouble was on the way. He feared what Jim might do to that person.

    C.J. said as they were talking he had no idea where they were going. They seemed to be headed toward Shelby. As they walked up the highway, Jim tried to hitch a ride for them. But no one stopped for them. C.J. became afraid and started praying to the Lord that nobody would stop for them. They walked a little farther, and Jim decided to turn back and go home. Right to this day, C.J. says he did not know where they were going, what Jim had on his mind, or what he was going to do. When they walked back to Mound Bayou, Jim told C.J. that he wanted him to go somewhere else with him the next day. C.J. agreed to go by telling him okay. They separated and C.J. went home. He stayed up for a while and went to bed. Jim was tired and got some rest.

    Jim got up the next morning and went somewhere. He was always on the move going somewhere. He visited some of his friends. I believe he felt lonely because some of his friends were not around.

    The next morning, July 14, 1965, Jim ate breakfast, took a bath, put on his clothes, and went somewhere. I don't know the place where he went. He didn't stay home too long. Around 1:00 pm, C.J. was supposed to come over and go somewhere with Jim. C.J. didn't show up. Jim got me to walk with him over to Pee Wee's house. C.J. was not home. So, we continued to walk over to where the Shannon boys live and around by the baseball field looking for C.J. Jim was very upset because C.J. didn't show up liked he had promised. I could hear him talking to himself. Then Jim asked me if I knew where C.J. was. I told him that I didn't know. When we turned around to go back home, coming back toward the Shannon house I saw C.J., Pee Wee, and the Shannon twin, Junior and Joe. They saw us and jumped over into a ditch to hide from us. Jim didn't see them at all. I didn't tell him what I had seen because he was already angry with C.J. for not showing up.

When we got home, Jim sat around for a while and told Mama he was going to find C.J. He went back over to where C.J. was living and found him at home. He told C.J. that he waited on him. C.J. told him that he was resting and fell asleep. C.J. walked Jim back to the house. Before C.J. went back home, he told Jim he didn't want to go with him because he had a feeling that something wasn't right. He was afraid for him. He mentioned the last time they were together and how Jim didn't tell him where they were going or what his plans were. He didn't know what to expect. C.J. told Jim he was going home and would see him around 5:00 pm.

When he left, Jim told Mama to wake him up at 5:00 pm. At 5:00 pm Mama woke Jim up. Jim noticed that C.J. had not returned as promised. He didn't show up. Jim asked his little brother Earnest to stick around because he wanted him to go somewhere with him. Jim ate, took him a bath, and put on a light grey pair of pants and a two tone shirt with light blue and grey. His shoes were light grey. He looked nice. While he was dressing, Mama and Grandmother went out on the porch and sat down.

I sat down and talked with him. He wanted me and Earnest to go with him in the morning to the cotton field to work. It was fine with me, but I told him they would not let me get on the truck. Jim gave me his word that nobody was going to mess with me. He told me to stay out of the street and stay around the house. He told me he didn't want to hurt anybody if they put their hands on me. I told him okay.

As tears rolled down my face, I kept saying that nobody was going to mess with me. He looked at me and saw me crying, and he wanted to know what was wrong. I told him nothing was wrong. Then he wanted to know why I was crying, and if he had hurt my feelings. I told him he did not hurt my feelings and I didn't know why I was crying. He told me to stop crying because nobody was going to mess with me.

Before he left out the door, he looked back and told me not to cry because everything was going to be all right. I got up and followed him to the door. He walked out on the porch and told Mama and Grandmother he would see them later.

As he and Earnest walked up the road, I continued to observe them. Suddenly he turned around and came back to the house. He must have forgotten something. He came in the house and got whatever he had left, and he gave me a dollar bill and a rain scarf. He told me to stop crying he would see me later. Again, I watched him and Earnest walk away until they got out of sight.

Earnest said that when they saw Daniel Toole sitting in his parked car, Jim asked Daniel if he could borrow his car for a while. Mr. Toole said something smart and it upset Jim. Jim pulled Mr. Toole from his car and knocked him to the ground. Earnest didn't remember what else was said.

Mr. Robinson told me that the reason Jim hit Mr. Daniel Toole was because he wouldn't loan him his car. Mr. Toole questioned Jim about his own car. Wasn't he just released from prison? That's when Jim struck him in the mouth. Earnest said after Jim pulled Mr. Toole out of the car, they drove off and went to Cleveland. They rode around in the car.

Mr. Toole went to Chief Byrd Isomer and told what Jim had done to him. Chief Byrd Isomer told Mr. Toole that he wasn't going have anything to do with this situation and to report it to the captain in Cleveland. He assured him that they would handle it. A highway patrolman came and picked up Mr. Toole, and they rode around looking for the car.

While they were driving in Cleveland, a police officer came up behind Jim and Earnest and ordered Jim to stop. Somehow he ditched the police on their way back to Mound Bayou. Earnest said that Jim was driving fast and he asked him to slow down, but it was too late. They turned over in the ditch. No one was hurt, and they got out of the car. Jim removed his shot gun from the car.

They started walking down the road. As they walked, Jim started praying to the Lord asking for help. Earnest told him not to worry, things were going to get better, and God would help him.

They walked on and got into another car. It was between eight and nine at night. They rode down a dark road out in the country near Moody Road. Earnest couldn't remember where they were going when the police came up behind them and turned their lights on. Jim slowed down and pulled back off. That point was when the police shot through the back window of the car and blew the whole window out. Jim stopped that time and no one was hurt.

The policed drove up and told them to get out of the car with their hands up. It was only one police officer and Daniel Toole. Mr. Toole told the officer which one was Willie Woodson because the officer didn't know what he looked like. Jim looked over at Earnest and told him to stand back.

When the police officer pulled out of his handcuffs, Jim was told to put his hands behind him. When Jim turned around very quickly, he knocked the policeman down to the ground and started kicking him. During the struggle, he took the policeman's gun. Then Daniel Toole jumped on Jim's back, but Jim managed to get him off and started beating up on him.

Jim told Earnest to run home and not tell anybody. Earnest ran a distance, looked back, and heard a gunshot. Then he started running faster and didn't stop until he got home. He had his muddy shoes in his hands. He got in bed with his muddy feet and didn't say a word to Mama or anybody about what had happened. Then he pretended he was asleep. Mama questioned him about Jim's whereabouts. Mama really wanted to know where he was. Earnest didn't say a word and continued faking like he was asleep. Mama begin to get worried, and she felt Jim was in trouble. Her and Grandmother stayed up until Jim walk in the door.

When Jim walked in the door, he had his shirt in his hand and threw it over in the chair. He sat down for a few minutes. He didn't have any shoes on because he left them behind. He didn't change clothes, but he kept on the same ones. He asked Mama if Earnest was all right. She told him that he was over there in the bed sleeping

Then he told Mama and Grandmother what had happened. He told them that he beat up a policeman and Daniel Toole. He showed Mama the policeman's gun that he had taken during the struggle. He told Mama he had to get away before they found him and he was going to try to leave town. He expressed that if they caught him that they were going to kill him. He told them to listen to the news and see if they hound him. He picked up his shirt and left the house, running without any shoes on his feet. He didn't tell anyone where he was going.

Everyone else in the family was still asleep. I had no knowledge of Jim's coming home and leaving quickly. I was asleep when Mama and Grandmother left the house.

I heard voices outside and someone was calling Willie Woodson's name. They were telling him to come out, or they were coming in. I had no idea it was the police. They repeated

Willie Woodson's name again and again and asked him to come out or they were going to come in. I got out of bed, went and opened the front door, and saw police everywhere. I saw one Black police officer, Chief Byrd Isomer. Their guns pointed at me and were ready to shoot. They told me to tell Willie Woodson to come out and give himself up, or they were going to come in. I told them that Willie Woodson was not inside. One of the police officers asked me if he could come in and search the house. Being a child and afraid, I told him yes. Two of the officers entered the house. They didn't have to look far because my grandmother lived in a two-room house.

While the other policemen stayed outside, they search the kitchen. I was asked by one of them about my parents. I told them that I didn't know. He wanted to know when the last time I saw Willie Woodson was and what he was wearing. I told him that I saw him yesterday and that he was wearing a black shirt and black pants. They told me that he had jumped on a police officer and Daniel Toole. They wanted him to give himself up.

Then they shined the flashlight down on the children while they were sleeping. He told me to turn the light on. I told him we didn't have any lights. I explained that Grandmother burned oil lamps. We were living in her two-bedroom after we moved back to Mound Bayou from Clinton.

Again, they asked me about my Mama and Daddy's location. I told them that I didn't know. They searched around the house and under the house. I saw one Black police officer out there from Mound Bayou. He was Chief Byrd Isomer. When they got through talking me, searching the house and all around the neighborhood looking for Jim, they left.

A few minutes later, Mama and Grandmother came to the house. I started telling them the police had been here. They said they saw the police and hid from them until they left the house.

Then Mama started telling me what Jim had done. They had gone to try to get somebody to help get Jim out of town. The person they were looking for was Mr. John Henry. He was out of town on a business trip. I told Mama everything the policeman said and that they planned to return.

Mama and Grandmother got up and went outside. They swept all around and mopped the porch to remove the footprints.

Some of the policemen came back that night looking for Jim. They talked to Mama and she told them she hadn't seen her son since yesterday. They told Mama that Jim had beat up one of their officers and taken his gun, and they wanted it back. Mama told them she hadn't seen him and didn't know where he was. They told Mama that he needed to give himself up and the gun also. They told her somebody was with him. And they left. They rode up and down our street and throughout the neighborhood all night long.

When they came back early that morning, they brought their dogs and searched around the yard for Jim's footprints. The dogs walked up and down the street, but they were unable to trace his footprints. The police told Mama that Willie Woodson had somebody with him, and they believed it was John Joe. Mama told them that Joe was out of town and couldn't be found.

They called somebody and found out it was Earnest who was with Jim, so they wanted to know where he was. Mama told them he was in the bed sleeping over there. They pulled the cover off Earnest and the rest of the children. They wanted to know which one was Earnest. Mama pointed him out, and they told Earnest to get up because they wanted to talk to him. Earnest acted as if he was very sleepy, but he was also afraid.

He got up and talked to the police officers. They asked him if he was with this brother the night he jumped on the police officer and Daniel Toole. Earnest told them no because he never went any place with his brother Jim. The police officer told Earnest that Daniel Toole and a police officer said that one of Woodson's brothers was with him.

Earnest's first story remained the same. He did not change his story. Then they asked about his shoes because they saw mud on his feet. Earnest told them he didn't have any shoes because his mother couldn't afford to buy him any. Suddenly they saw some muddy shoes underneath the bed and wanted to know who they belonged to. Earnest told them they belonged to his little brother, T.W. They asked Earnest to try the shoe on. When he tried it on, it didn't fit his feet. The police saw for themselves that it didn't fit. What they didn't know was that Earnest had his toes drawn up in the shoes to make it not fit properly.

They told Mama that they wanted to take Earnest down to the police station for further questioning. Earnest said when he arrived at the station, the strategy they used on him was scaring him with the dog. They wanted to make him tell where Jim was hiding, but he didn't tell them anything.

Earnest's identity was revealed by a police officer at the questioning. The police who Jim had beat up recognized Earnest. He told the other officers that Earnest was the one who was with his brother. Earnest denied that he was the brother with Jim that night. He repeatedly told them that it wasn't him. They told him stop lying or they were going to put their dog on him. Earnest told them that he was not lying. After he didn't him tell the truth, they left him alone.

The policeman Jim beat up had a bandage around his head and another on one of his hands. He told Earnest that his brother was very strong and that he had a bad brother. He also told him that if they caught Jim, they were going to kill him. After that, Earnest couldn't remember anything else and they brought him back home.

Police officers were still searching everywhere, going back and forward over to Mr. Frank's house, looking for Willie and questioning C.J. and other people.

The police kept coming back to the house and questioning us if Willie had been there and if he had left their gun. They told Mama and Grandmother not to leave the house because they would be watching the house. They told her they would be back and would take her down for questioning also.

When they left, I saw tears in my mother's eyes. They wanted her to tell where her son was hiding out. My mother didn't know where he had gone when he left the house running. My mother was six or eight months pregnant. Her hands were full. She was not feeling well, and her nose bled. I was so angry with the policemen, and I wanted them to leave her alone. I wanted to say something, but Mama told me not to say anything because they were already angry.

Policemen were riding and looking for Jim, telling everybody that when they found him he would be a dead nigger.

The policemen came back and told Mama that they had gotten a call saying that Willie was in Greenwood, living with our cousin O.W. Steward. They wanted to know if she had an address on O.W. Steward.

My grandmother told them she did not know his address. She kept all of her letters and papers inside of her chifforobe. Then they wanted to see what she was hiding in it. Grandmother tried to explain to them that only her clothes and important papers were in it. It was locked. They wanted her to unlock it so they could see what was inside it. She didn't want to open it, and Mama told her to go get the key, Grandmother had the key down inside her purse hidden in the kitchen beside the stove. The policemen followed her into the kitchen as she was getting the keys. She opened up the chifforobe. All they found was her clothes and letters from her sister and other relatives. They took all her things and poured them on the porch to go through them. The found out an address for O.W. and got in touch with O.W. Steward. They found out that Jim had never been in Greenwood.

When they didn't find anything, they got in their cars and told Grandmother to pick up her own damn paper. They left all of Grandmother's things on the porch for her to pick up. They told Mama she better not leave the house because they were watching her and if she saw her son to tell him to leave their gun.

While they were gone, C.J. came over and talked to Mama alone. He told her he had seen Jim and where he was hiding. He told Mama he walked out on the back porch to throw out the dish water and heard someone calling his name. He looked down and it was Jim looking up at him from underneath the house. He told Jim to come on inside the house. He came in, sat down, and told him what he had done. He told C.J. that he had beaten up a police officer and Daniel Toole. He knew he was in trouble.

Jim told C.J. he had taken the policeman's gun. He showed the gun to him. He told C.J. that during the struggle, Jim took his gun and tried to shoot him, but the gun wouldn't go off. After that, he took off running, leaving his shoes behind, and came home to tell Mama what had happened. He didn't tell anyone where he was going. C.J. said Jim told him to clean the gun up for him because it had mud on it. He told C.J. he was going to leave town. C.J. tried to convince him to give himself up. Jim told C.J. there no way he was going to turn himself in or go back to jail. He wasn't going to let the police beat him up and put him back in jail either. He told C.J. as soon as everything cleared, he was going to leave town. C.J. said that Jim was afraid and nervous, so C.J. was going to help him escape. He asked Jim if he was hungry and Jim said yes.

C.J. walked down to Mr. Dick Battle's grocery store and bought some eggs and bacon and cooked some for Jim.

Jim told C.J. to go and check on the family. Jim went back under the house when he got through talking. Later on, C.J. came over and told Mama where Jim was hiding. He was under Pee Wee's house. He gave Jim a blanket to lie on while he was underneath the house. C.J. told Mama he going back home to watch for him. Jim wanted C.J. to wake him up at 3:00 pm.

The news had spread all over town, and through the town they set up road blocks to make sure Jim didn't leave before they caught him.

Mama got somebody to take Grandmother and me over to Mr. John Henry's house to see if he had come back from out of town. He worked with the NAACP. On our way to his house, the police pulled us over and made us get out of the car. They asked the man to open his trunk; they found nothing and let us go

When we got to Mr. Henry's house, he was not at home. So, we came back home. The police officers took Mama away with them. She was forced to get into the car, and they rode her around, talking bad to her. During the time she was in the car, she took a lot of abuse—cursing, beating, and name calling—while she was in their custody. Though she wouldn't tell them where her son was, they drove around town asking her all types of questions, and they called her all kind of names. They questioned her about her son and tried to make her tell where Jim was, but she kept telling them that she didn't know. They told her that she ought to stop lying. The told her that she was a lying Black bitch and she better tell the truth. They told her they knew about the two cars he had taken and his bad-ass reputation on the street and how he tried to be a bad son of a bitch. They kept saying bad things to her.

They told her they had his shoes in the trunk of their damn car. The police went and got the shoes and showed them to her. They wanted to know if the shoes were Jim's. Mama told them she didn't know. They called her a lying bitch. They told her if she saw her son that she should encourage him to turn himself in. But if they caught him, he was a dead son of a bitch. They stressed that they wanted to get the gun back.

They asked Mama about her husband. She told them that he was dead. One policeman told her that it was good because Daddy was a dirty black N— going around trying to get people to vote. They said he should have been dead a long time ago. Mama said they asked her how she was going to take care of all those damn children. She told them she was going to take care of her children. One police officer told her she was a smartass black bitch and hit her in the mouth with his hand, knocking out two teeth. One was a gold tooth. They constantly harassed her. She was told she may as well tell them where Jim was because they were not going to give up until they found him. Mama said one of the officers told the other officers they might as well let this black bitch out of the car because she might not know where her son was.

When Mama walked in the house, blood was all over her mouth and she had tears in her eyes. A cold chill came all over me, and tears started rolling down my eyes. I ran out of the house and down the street because I didn't know what to do. I walked up town and over to where C.J. lived. I was walking and praying. I told C.J. what had happened to Mama. I asked C.J. if he had seen Jim. He told me no and to go back home and see about Mama. When I got back home, Grandmother was sitting there and talking to Mama. I was so angry I asked Mama which of the officers did that to her. She told me not to say anything to them because they were already angry.

Rev. Robinson told me those in charge had gotten another inmate from prison to help hunt for Jim. They solicited help from all kinds of people, and anyone who wanted to join in the hunt were welcomed. The hunted him like an animal. They town's people were afraid and didn't know what to do. The police asked them if they had seen Jim.

Mr. Lewis Hawkins told me that the police had come to his house the night he had gotten in trouble. Willie Lewis didn't know Jim was in trouble. They put their guns in his face and demanded he tell them where Willie was. The tips to the police were false. The police told Lewis somebody had told them they had seen him and Willie together the night before at one of those clubs. Lewis repeated the same thing over and over again, that he hadn't seen Jim. Then the police started talking about shooting Lewis if he didn't tell them the truth.

They had their guns all in his face. They soon left him alone. Lewis said the police car was running hot and smoking, and he could tell they were tired of driving and looking for Willie. Lewis said he watched those police riding down the street all over Mound Bayou. He said they were stopping people and making them get out of their cars to lie on the ground. Lewis said he never saw so many angry policemen in his life. It was actually a mob. He said he would never forget that day. He remembered my brother as a good friend who had a good heart and didn't take mess off anyone.

There were some plans of escape from C.J. and other people. C.J. and others planned to sneak Jim out of town that night. Other people planned to put Jim in a casket and take his body to another town. People had all types of plans for him.

The police were going back and forth to Mr. Frank's house looking for Jim. C.J. lived with Mr. Frank and his sons. Somebody tipped the police that Jim had a brother that lived there. They stopped to talk to C.J. and Pee Wee. The police told them that if they caught Jim, he would be a dead N—. They told the police that they hadn't see him. Then the police left and started riding up and down the Bank Addition Community. That was where we lived and where Jim was hiding out

The policemen were everywhere, all out in the country stopping and searching people's cars. They wanted to search people's houses, but people would not let the police in to search. Rev. O.D. Robinson, pastor of New Hope Baptist Church in Mound Bayou, was a good friend of Jim's. He said that the police wanted to search his neighbor's house, but he would not let them in.

We were told that the policemen stopped cars and forced the people get out to lie on the ground, and then they put their guns up their noses and questioned them. They tried to make people stay in their houses. They were not giving up on their search for Jim, and they even thought he had already left town.

I walked twice over to where C.J. was living. I asked him if he had seen Jim, and he told me no. I left him and came home. I walked around and prayed, hoping that they would never find him. The police officers offered people money to tell where Jim was hiding.

Two of Rev. Robinson's neighbors knew where Jim was hiding. They saw C.J. looking under the house and talking to somebody. They told Rev. Rudolph, and he asked his neighbors specific details of how they knew it was Jim. The told him they had seen one of his sisters coming over there, C.J. looking under the house, someone moving around underneath the house, and Jim looking out from under the house. It was two twin houses sitting side by side. One was green and the other was red. Jim was under the red house.

So, Rev. Rudolph went and tipped Chief Byrd Isomer off about Jim's hideout. He gave him the same information that his neighbors had given him. Chief Byrd Isomer and Rev. Rudolph told Sheriff Capps. The police questioned him about the certainty of the location and how he knew. He repeated the same information over again. They questioned him more and more as he divulged Jim's hiding place. We were told they offered him money to tell where that N— was hiding. Rev. Robinson said that it about $20.00, but no one knows for sure.

It was between three and four o' clock. C.J. left the house and walked down to the store to get Jim something to eat. It was time for C.J. to wake Jim up, around three o' clock. While he was at the store, Rev. Robinson recalled it was about 3:00 pm or after that the mob with guns and dogs headed for that house. They came in all types of cars.

The police knocked on Pee Wee's door and asked him about Willie. He told them that he was not there. He then went back to his room and stretched out on his bed. The police surrounded the house.

C.J. was coming out of the store, saw all the policemen around his house, and realized that they had found Jim. He headed towards that way running, but Mr. Dicks Battle grabbed him and threw him to the ground. He held him there. C.J. tried to get away from Mr. Battle.

The police told people to get back into their houses, but they wouldn't go. Some stayed on their front porches and watched it live. Rev. Robinson said that Jim was hunted like animal.

Rev. Robinson was a law enforcement officer at that time. Rev. Robinson even asked if he could go and talk to Willie about giving himself up because they were good friends. He believed he could talk to Willie about coming out. One of the officers asked Chief Byrd Isomer who Rev. Robinson was. Chief Byrd Isomer told them he was a trained law enforcement officer and a private investigator. Rev. Robinson's request was denied. Chief Capp told everybody to stand back and not to get any closer because Jim had a gun under the house.

The Mississippi Highway Patrolman M.E. Lamas was widely known by the citizens of Mound Bayou as a ruthless, bloodthirsty policeman. He approached the house, got down on his knees, and called Jim a N—. He ordered him to come out from under the house and told him he was dead N— anyway. "Come out you N—." All the other officers were down on their knees, looking at him under the house. A shot was fired. I don't know who fired the shot first. It was said two officers were shot, and one was shot five times.

We don't know who fired the first shot. When they saw one of their men shot, they went crazy. They rushed to the house and started firing their guns. They reached under the house and dragged Jim out.

When I was walking from up town on my way back over to Mr. Frank's house to talk to C.J., I heard those machine guns. I started running faster, and I met my friend Wilma coming from that direction. She told me they found my brother, and I told her that I already knew. I started running towards the crowd and could hear machine guns firing. Mr. Tommie Hearon grabbed hold of me and wouldn't let me go. I wanted to see my brother as I screamed and cried. I saw people crying and hollering. I heard them say that they killed that boy. Rev. Robinson said that after he was pulled from under the house, all one hundred of them opened fire and kept firing. They just kept shooting and reloading and reloading every time one of Jim's muscles would jump or move. The fired into him again. Sheriff Capps was yelling for them to hold their fire on the bullhorn, but they just kept shooting. They beat him across the head with their sticks.

Jim was unrecognizable when the shooting stopped. People watched in horror from their porches. Jim's body from his waist up was torn open, and his vital organs lay on the ground in a bloody mass of flesh. His heart, liver, and brain lay on the ground. His face was torn off, and his stomach was shot up. They beat him with their sticks.

The two officers were shot. Rev. Robinson said that as they carried away the two officers in the helicopter, one died. It never was told how the officers were shot. I believe they were shot by their on men.

Rev. Robinson said that as they carried away the two officers, they told the people, "Y'all get that N— up." After the mob left, it was said one of the officers was shot by their own men. I saw them pick Jim off the ground and put him in a plastic bag and into the ambulance.

When the shooting started, Pee Wee said he jumped out of bed and ran to the back of the house. Bullets were coming in through the walls. He ran back to his bedroom and got down on the floor. He crawled under the bed and hid under there until the shooting stopped. He was afraid and looked out the window, and he saw Jim laying in a pool of blood. His face was torn up after the shooting stopped.

When all gunfire ceased, I ran down to that house and saw Mama, Grandmother, C.J., and other people standing there, looking at Jim's body parts. One of the Norwood men buried his body parts in the ground next to that house.

There were so many people standing around watching Jim get shot up by the police and mob. People and children were standing there crying. Mama, Grandmother, and I left the scene and walked on back to the house. Then we walked up town to the funeral home to see Jim's body. Mama and Grandmother went in, but I did not follow them because I couldn't and started crying. The man that ran the funeral home told me not to go in there. As I stood outside and waited on Mama and Grandmother, C.J. walked up and asked me if Mama and Grandmother were inside. I told him they were inside the funeral home. He wanted to know if I was coming inside, and I told him no. I didn't want to go in.

There were so many people going in to view his body and show their respect. Everyone came out crying and holding their stomachs, head, and mouths. Someone came out, and told me Mama fainted twice in the funeral home.

When they came out, she asked me what happened to me and why I didn't come in. I told her I couldn't and I didn't want to see Jim like that, all shot up. As we walked back home Mama continued to talk and cry. She told me she couldn't stand looking at her son all shot up. His head was busted wide open with his brain sticking out, and half of his face was torn apart. His legs and feet were shot up, and Jim was stretched out with one hand up. He was covered up with a white sheet, and the only things Mama took from his body were his two rings and my watch.

She told the funeral home man that she wanted his clothes, and they agreed to give them to her. When we made it home, she told me she wanted me to stay with the other children. She and Grandmother rode the Greyhound bus to Cleveland to see Mr. Amzie Moore and tell him about what they had done to her son. As soon as they were gone, I left the house and told my little sister Annie and the rest of the children to stay in the house until I came back. When I returned, she told me a car full of white guys pulled up in the yard and blew their horn. She peeked out the window and saw one of them on the porch. He blew through the door and said a racial remark. "You N—, when we come back, you better not be there!" After that, I remained home until Mama and Grandmother returned. We told Mama what had happened while they were gone.

Mama told me she had talked with Mr. Amzie Moore. He told her he had heard the police were looking for someone, but he didn't know who that person was. He told her if she had gotten in touch with him right away, they would have stopped them before it took place. She told him she couldn't leave the house because the police ordered her not to leave and they were watching her. She told him that she did not have the money to bury her son.

He told her to go down to the police station and tell them that they all killed him and were the ones that needed to bury him because we didn't have any money to bury him. Mama and Grandmother left Mr. Moore's home to go to the police station. When they were walking down the street near the police station, they heard them talking amongst themselves that they had just killed a N— in Mound Bayou. They went on inside of the police station and gave them the message Mr. Moore had sent, saying that they killed her son and should bury him because she didn't have any insurance or money. Somehow they agreed to bury him.

Jim's body was sent to Mark, Mississippi. They couldn't hold his body out any longer because the fluid wouldn't stay in him. He was shot up so badly, Mama didn't have any choice but to bury him right away. She didn't have enough time to contact anybody, and Mama set his burial a little early, July 17, 1965.

On Friday, July 17, 1965, when we got ready for the burial, I couldn't find the mate to my other shoe. I had everything laid out for the burial. I couldn't find my shoe. We looked everywhere for my shoe. But we couldn't find it, and everyone went to the funeral except me and Earnest. He hid himself from everyone because he was afraid the police were coming back for him. I sat on the porch and cried the whole time they were gone until they came back. A man walked by the house and tried to get me to go inside.

I sat there on the porch until the family came back from the burial. Jim's body was taken from the funeral home to the graveyard. He was placed in a plastic bag and buried in a wooden box. He was buried in one of Daddy's suits. They didn't have any church service, and there wasn't a preacher around at the gravesite. They just laid him to rest. Mama fell out twice while watching them put her son down in the ground. People started crying. They were sad and hurting all at the same time. I wanted to see my brother before they put him down in the ground. He was buried in a wooden box, no casket was what I was told.

After the funeral, you couldn't see anybody on the street. It was a sad day. My mother was pregnant at the time, between five and six months. I was sad because I wasn't there to watch them as they laid Jim's body to rest. Earnest was sad because he wasn't present either. We found out he was under the bed and afraid the policemen were going to be there.

It was sad for Mama because she was hurt. She wasn't given enough time to make any arrangement to have a funeral for her dead son. Also, she wasn't able to contact anybody. Our cousin O.W. and his son came down for the funeral. But Mama buried him away right because his body wouldn't hold fluid.

Jim's friends were on their way to Mound Bayou from out of town, and they had an accident and didn't make it to the funeral. Plus, they didn't know when or where the funeral was going to be. They were very hurt over Jim's death.

People were never the same from that day on. They took it hard at his burial, and they said they would never forget that day. After the burial, Mama and Grandmother went back to Cleveland to let Mr. Amzie Moore know the family was being threatened. He told her to go back and pack her things. He was going to send someone to move us away from Mound Bayou and not to tell anyone. That night while we were packing our things, I found my other shoe down on the floor by the bed. We don't know how that shoe got there.

Late in the evening, the NAACP came to pick us up. We didn't take anything except the clothes we had on our backs. We had to leave everything behind. They took us to a place called Mount Bullah, Mississippi. We were among white and black civil rights workers. Very nice people, they helped the family out a lot. They gave us money and clothes. We had never heard of that town before. The people in Mound Bayou didn't know where we went.

I remember a few white men who came to Mama and talked to her about her son's death. They wanted to help her, but she needed witnesses. They told her they examined Jim's body, and he was shot more than 150 times and had a fractured skull. They told Mama if she could get somebody to be a witness for her, they could take a case to court. They told her it was wrong for them to shoot him up like that.

Mama and I went to Mound Bayou. She wanted to talk to a few people. It was hard for them to talk about Jim's death because they were afraid the mob would come back and do something to them. Mama couldn't get one person to be a witness for her. The NAACP wanted to help her.

Mama and I returned back to Mound Bullah. We were told that people had taken sick after Jim's death because they had never seen anybody get shot up like that before.

Joe came home from Florida looking for us. He was unaware of the things that had happened to the family. He told C.J. he had a bad a dream that something bad had happened and something told him he needed to go home. He got up the next morning and caught the Greyhound bus back to Mound Bayou. C.J. explained everything that had happened. Joe fainted. Joe took it very hard. C.J. called Mama and told her he was putting Joe on the bus. The NAACP met Joe at the bus station.

Joe cried about his brother's brutal death. Mama and Grandmother had a hard time getting Joe to stop crying. He really was hurt to come home and hear the bad news about his daddy's and brother's deaths. We understood how he felt.

My mama and grandmother were strong Christian women. They prayed all the time, and they looked after each other. My grandmother stood by her daughter through hard times.

The civil rights people asked Mama to select another environment. They wanted to know what city or town she selected. Mama told them Memphis, Tennessee. Someone got in touch with a man named Grove C. Burson to help us out once we got there. They moved us on October 3, 1965.

When we got settled down, Mama went to see somebody about her son's death. Whoever that person was told her if she could go back to Mound Bayou and get witnesses, they would take it to court. Mama talked to a few people and they didn't want to get involved. So, she gave up and left it alone.

Mama, Grandmother, and I got our cousin Ernestine to take us back to Mound Bayou every now and then to visit Jim's grave. One lady told me her son took sick after seeing someone shot up so bad.

Right now to this day, it hurts C.J. when I ask him questions about Jim. He gets upset and tells me that he doesn't want to talk about it and to leave it alone. Later, I would approach him again with questions, and he would tell me he doesn't want to remember. C.J. and Jim were very close.

Jim was close to the family. I believe on the day of the incident, Jim was very troubled within. He couldn't shake it off. When a person is troubled inside, it can lead to anything. The day he went to Daniel Toole for his car, he had never bothered or even said anything to that man before or done anything out of the way to him. Jim always gave Mr. Daniel Toole respect. I know he was troubled. He couldn't handle his unmanageable emotions.

I would like to express my personal feelings of displeasure about the apprehension Jim. People questioned Mayor Wesley Liddell of Mound Bayou for his lack of judgment or thought in the whole ordeal. He gave the outside police force the right to come in and do what they wanted to do. He should have told them that the law enforcement of Mound Bayou would be responsible for bringing Jim in, and that would have avoided the whole incident.

As a result, this left the town divided. Friends, neighbors, relatives, and various church denominations were all upset at the mayor's decision. I was very angry with the mayor until the day he died. Each time I came down to Mound Bayou with my mother, I would see him sitting in a chair on the corner. I just stood there watching him, and I wanted to go and say something to him. I thought about my brother C.J. and what he told me about not saying nothing to those people in Mound Bayou. Mayor Wesley never did have a peace of mind, and the people didn't vote for him again.

Rev. Rudolph and Byrd Isomer were equally responsible for something unjustly done. After Rev. Rudolph notified Chief Byrd Isomer of Jim's location, they both told the outside police force who had invaded Mound Bayou at that time. This situation could have been handled differently. Their hands have blood on them for the part they played in Jim's death. The same blood is on all others' hands who secretly participated in Jim's demise.

I believed another example of Jim's unmanageable emotions was when a highway patrolman called Jim the N-word and told him that he was a dead anyway. I believed this triggered him. This caused him to open fire. His emotions were racing inside of him. He knew they had a hatred for him. He knew they were going to kill him. So, someone made the first shot, and one of the officers was shot five times. He was rushed to the hospital and later died.

The people in Mound Bayou had plans on how they were going to handle the situation, secret plans to help Jim escape, but somebody knew where he was. The people were willing to put their lives and reputations on the line so justice could be served fairly. One plot was to hide Jim in a casket and drive him across the state line to freedom so the police couldn't capture him. They knew deep down in their hearts that he would not serve a short time at that time. The daily court system was inadequate. Something happened in the town, and nothing was said about it. For example, the prominent citizens' crimes were kept quiet and the local citizens' crimes were prosecuted.

Jim's death was never mentioned unless it dealt with the investigation of the highway patrolman's death. Nothing was said anymore of Jim's death.

The betrayal of Willie Woodson left Rev. Rudolph a hated man throughout the town. He didn't have any friends. The whole town disliked him. That included the children. Whenever they would see him on the street, they would throw things at him and call him names. It was said that he would go to Cleveland and tell the police what they had done to him. The police would send threatening messages by Rev. Rudolph to the people of Mound Bayou and throughout the town about his harassment.

My sister-in-law told me that when Rev. Rudolph would go places, he used to flag a car down for somebody to pick him up and give him a ride. After the betrayal of Jim, people refused to stop and give him a ride.

Rev. Robinson said his mother went to Rev. Rudolph and questioned him about telling on Jim. His response was that somebody told him where Jim was hiding and reported to the police. And he did not request it. Rev. Robinson's mother told him that he ought to be ashamed of himself and he had to answer to the Lord for what he had one. He told her that he should have been dead and needed to be dead.

Mrs. Broomfield told me that she got on Rev. Rudolph's case about telling on that young man. She told him he ran his mouth too much when he went to the police and it was a disgrace. Rudolph told her that he didn't regret it at all, not one day. I was told how Rudolph died. Some said he was poisoned to death, and some said he died in his house, sitting there with his girlfriend.

Many witnesses who still remain have not forgotten that terrible day. I know in my heart that Earth hath no sorrow that heaven cannot heal. As years have passed, many hearts have forgiven the unjust wrong of that day. This is what it is about. We have to forgive if we want to be forgiven. This incident will live on in the lives of all who remember that day. Right to this day, the people in Mound Bayou are still angry and upset about the police coming in to their town and killing a Black man.

All the mayors of Mound Bayou, starting with Mayor Wesley Liddell, have never given an apology to the Woodson family for the way Jim was apprehended. No promises have been made to never allow this to happen again in this all-Black town. This will not bring Jim back, but it will give the citizens a sense of security and protection from those in authority in time of a crisis. The Woodson family has forgiven all authorities for that unforgettable day.

Sad to say, my brother did not want it to end this way. He never got a chance to live out his dreams. He wanted to be a boxer, get married, and take care of his family. He never got a chance to do the things he wanted to do. He never got a chance to come out from under the house. I believe that Jim never wanted to die at that early age. I know he had a good heart and was a good person.

www.ingramcontent.com/pod-product-compliance
Lightning Source LLC
Chambersburg PA
CBHW080637230426

43663CB00016B/2905